STELLA'S KITCHEN

Creative Cooking for Fun, Flavor and a Lean, Strong Body

By Stella C. Juarez

Foreword by
Dave Draper

On Target Publications
Aptos, California, USA

STELLA'S KITCHEN

Creative Cooking for Fun, Flavor and a Lean, Strong Body
By Stella C. Juarez

Copyright © 2003, Stella C. Juarez
First printing March 2003
ISBN: 1-931046-89-1

Published by:
On Target Publications
P. O. Box 1335
Aptos, CA 95001 USA
(888) 466-9185
info@ontargetpublications.com
www.ontargetpublications.com

Foreword by Dave Draper

Library of Congress Cataloging-in-Publication Data

Juarez, Stella C., 1974-
  Stella's kitchen : creative cooking for fun, flavor, and a lean,
strong body / by Stella C. Juarez ; foreword by Dave Draper.
     p. cm.
Includes bibliographical references and index.
 ISBN 1-931046-89-1
 1. Cookery. I. Title.
 TX714 .J83 2003
 641.5—dc21

                              2002151879

Disclaimer: Every effort has been made to verify the information in this book. Should any errors or omissions be discovered, they will be corrected in subsequent printings.

Acknowledgements

First and foremost, I give thanks to my Almighty God and Father for protecting me through all of my life's twists and turns. You have blessed my life with an immeasurable wealth of good family, true friends, and teachers who all cared enough to believe in me.

My sincere appreciation goes to Dave Draper for taking this leap of faith and leaving a path of footprints behind him on the way to the squat rack. My deep gratitude extends to his amazing and brilliant wife, Laree, for her editorial work and for making a dream I only joked about a reality.

Tearful thanks goes to my superman of a father for enduring years of endless "messes" in his kitchen and to my mom for her unconditional love. To the rest of my family, especially Olivia, David, Gina, and Dad, thank you for helping me raise my little boy over these last years and loving him like he was your own. Lastly, to my precious son, Isaiah, you've been a great little friend throughout every circumstance and challenge. You have taught me so much with your gentle acceptance of life's offerings and made me a better person. You are the crown jewel of my life's treasure chest.

—SJ

Table of Contents

Foreword by Dave Draper

Preface

Beef

1

Poultry

2

Fish Fare

Breakfast Basics

Protein Snacks

5

Vegetables

6

Safe Sauces

7

Kitchen Toolkit

8

Foreword

The food thing...We are more influenced by food than we are religion, politics, family and friends. A good meal outshines a sunny day. Conglomerates are formed, consequential disputes are settled and proposals of marriage are made over the gracious sharing of pleasurable food.

We eat everything from frankfurters to frogs and Snickers to snails. Food is in the air, in the seas, underground and grows on trees. It's everywhere. We can't live without food, yet because of our love affair with it, we severely compromise our health and shorten our lives. We eat downright bad foods, too much of the wrong foods and not enough of the right foods, and we eat in excess. Oh, boy, do we eat.

Now Stella is one of those remarkable individuals who has adored food all her life and, therefore, has centered her attention on its finer qualities, its taste, texture and fragrance, its preparation and its consumption. She has become an artisan in the kitchen.

Cooking is fun, but nothing compares to the eating.

Consumption of food became one of our author's more outstanding culinary accomplishments. Cooking and steaming, slicing and dicing are mute tasks if not accompanied by testing and tasting. Stella, during her years of passionate study and extensive practice, gained weight to match her broadening skill. The day came in Stella's life when food and its preparation looked back at her from the unkind mirror in the dining room. The young lady slipped into the over-sized category while braising duck in her secret honey-glaze.

In a race for priority, exercise gained the lead while creative cooking fell to a safe second. Walking and jogging led our determined heroine to marathon running and weight lifting, muscle and might. Stella is a warrior. She loves food no less and refuses to diet. She simply expelled the junk from her pantry, kitchen cupboards and bulging refrigerator. The troublemakers, bandits and thieves were last seen hanging out at the local landfill feeding the pigeons.

She emerged with the same brilliant passion for taste and creativity, but smothered it with purpose and sautéed it with loving care. Her thoughts: You eat to satisfy, delight and reward yourself, of course, but you eat to serve well your marvelous body and its needs. There is no joy at the expense of your health.

If you are a warrior, you will find protein-rich meals for muscle building, energy-packed snacks for high performance, pre-game power meals for the dynamic athlete, smart and constructive dishes for the heavyweight seeking a fighting weight and meaty feeds for the active lightweight striving for solid mass.

Simple, nutritious and mouth-watering quick fixes are on every other page for the taste-conscious, weight-conscious kitchen-lazy. There are daring, high-value meals to suit the fastidiously slim.

Unique kitchen tips and hints, food-processing cues and generous contributions of culinary wisdom add variety, ease and fascination to your kitchen and food preparation.

There are so many cookbooks on the market, who can count them? Stella's Kitchen spills over with imagination and simplicity, flavor and goodness. It's a book for the high performer and fit, the bright-spirited and enthusiastic, the creative who seeks superior health and long life, as well as the self-considerate and hungry... obviously, you.

Dave Draper
Mr. America, Mr. Universe
Author of Your Body Revival: Weight Loss Straight Talk

Preface

Perhaps no other person in the world requires a diet as nutritious as the athlete concerned with personal performance. We may see a professional athlete sprinting down a track, flexing his muscles on a stage or jumping over opponents to catch a pass in the end zone. We watch in silent awe as interconnecting mounds of muscle tissue fire with graceful power. We imagine how hard he must train to look like that and may visualize him doing bicep curls—teeth clenched, beads of sweat dripping down his temples. What we don't often stop to picture is the kind of food this athlete must consume to build and repair muscle tissue and otherwise maintain order in a talented body that produces chaos and destruction. Every recipe in this book represents a nod to the importance of eating a muscle-building, body-repairing diet while still living a normal life.

Whether or not you call yourself an "athlete," Stella's Kitchen: Creative Cooking for Fun, Flavor and a Lean, Strong Body" will teach you how to cook healthy, well-balanced meals for you and your family. The delicious recipes within will emphasize protein intake and the consumption of minimally-processed complex carbohydrates and de-emphasize the tradition of loading dishes with sodium and sugar.

If you're dieting or just looking for ways to clean up favorite dishes and reduce your sugar intake, I applaud your decision to defend your body against the illnesses, diseases, and deterioration that comes with poor food choices. If you are bold and willing to make small changes in your diet, my friend, you are different. Rather than bumble carelessly from one meal to the next, you care and understand that eating better is necessary for your long-term health and well-being. Grab an apron and let's turn away from the fast-food melee that's overcoming throngs of good people who should know better. You, you're different.

If you are a serious or recreational athlete of any sort, may this cookbook be a companion at your training table. I already know you are interested in eating food that will support the growth of lean muscle tissue while minimizing the preponderance of body fat. In fact, you see food as fuel that helps you meet strength, agility, speed or other physical improvement goals. You know nutritious food helps you recover from strenuous physical activities that you love and enables you to get up the next day to do them all over again. Since I know what's on most American dinner tables, I imagine you often find yourself eating separately from your friends and precious family. Put down that dumbbell. Hop off the treadmill. I've got something I want to show you.

Please note: This cookbook is not accompanied by a secret diet or training regimen. It's not part of the latest fad diet bandwagon nor will it send subliminal messages to you to purchase any specific product. While it is intended for an audience of busy athletes, the dishes are meant to please the palettes of those yet to discover the athlete within and the pessimists who never fathomed "eating right" could taste so good. This cookbook is a collection of recipes from a woman of strength who was practically born in the kitchen wearing a chef's hat and holding a big wooden spoon. As a consequence of my kitchen talent and a lack of knowledge about nutrition, I lived a chubby life and eventually found the bathroom scales occasionally tipping 203 pounds. I still enjoy good food and cooking for my family and loved ones. The difference now, aside from smaller clothes, is a genuine love for the power, strength and health that comes with living the inspired life of an athlete. What you hold in your hands is a collection of recipes that will hopefully encourage you to believe that good health and fine food and happiness go hand in hand.

There is, however, one common ingredient you'll need for every dish: Always cook with love. As you prepare these things, think about the people for whom you are cooking and imagine how this fresh and tasty food will nourish their bodies from the inside out. Cook from your soul the gift that will enable their bodies to pursue physical activity and athletic goals—big and small—that will keep them fired up about being alive. Let love, care and sweet thoughts swirl about, radiating through your fingertips as you slice and chop, even if you'll be the only one sitting at the table.

You've picked up more than a cookbook, friend. These recipes for energetic, health-conscious adults are truly enjoyable by people who could give a lick about nutrition. These recipes are simple and fast because I understand the need to spend hours in the kitchen may deter you from long-term dietary health. I know many of you may be trying to build a body on a shoestring budget, so I've included information from my own experiences as a single mother and an athlete to help you accomplish your dietary goals economically.

My sincere hope is that what you find here will inspire what may currently be a bland or unhealthy diet. Beyond this, I hope that it fuels a personal record here and there and even greater, that it will become a tool that helps you move forward in your quest for a healthier lifestyle year after year.

Stella Juarez
Colorado, USA

1

Beef

There are a lot more to ways to eat beef than just burgers and steaks. Many people who eat "lean" avoid beef because they are under the false impression that all beef is fattening, or they simply do not understand how to cook lean with beef. The truth is, the kind of beef served by drive-through restaurants has had a visibly negative impact on the health of the American public. This chapter can help you overcome thse dilemmas and will show you how to successfully incorporate beef into a healthy diet. Turn the page and learn how to cook the right cuts of beef and accompany them with wholesome side dishes.

1

Beef

Cook times in recipes have been reduced by one third since the recipes in this cookbook use USDA Lite or American Heart Association Heart Healthy beef which is leaner and cooks in less time than other beef.

Beef 101: Cooking Beef

One of the side benefits of cooking beef is how a simple alteration in cooking time changes how the steak will taste. No matter which cut you start off with, cooking for various lengths of time allows for great flexibility in preparing red meats. With a little know-how, you can be a gracious and considerate cook able to cook a steak that will please the palate of any guest.

These helpful hints will help you determine how well done your beef cuts will be.

	Feels	Temp °F	Looks	*Cook Time@350°F
RARE	slightly firmer than raw meat	120° at center	cool red center, red from edge to edge	15-25 minutes per pound
MEDIUM RARE	a little firmer than raw meat, has slight "give"	135° at center	warm red center slightly brown edges	20-30 minutes per pound
MEDIUM	firmer than raw meat, losing its "give"	150° at center	hot light pink center, brown at edges	25-35 minutes per pound
MEDIUM WELL	mostly firm	160° at center	hot, slightly pink center, brown throughout	30-35 minutes per pound
WELL	completely firm	165° at center	gray throughout	30-40 minutes per pound
PITTSBURGH	completely firm	170° at center	gray throughout blackened	35-40 minutes per pound

*Cook time calculations are based on a three-pound roast. Cook times have been reduced by one third since the recipes in this cookbook use USDA "Lite" or American Heart Association Heart Healthy beef which is leaner and cooks in less time than other beef.

4 servings

Ingredients

Fajitas

1 pound flank steak (or top round) cut in strips and pricked with fork

1 tablespoon light olive oil

4 cloves garlic

1 medium white onion, sliced

1 small green bell pepper, sliced

1 small red bell pepper, sliced

2 roma tomatoes, diced and set aside

Marinade

½ cup reduced-sodium soy sauce

1 tablespoon white wine or red wine vinegar

½ teaspoon ground ginger

3 cloves of garlic finely chopped

3 ounces light beer

1 tablespoon onion powder

3 tablespoons lime juice (reserved)

1 teaspoon cornstarch (reserved)

2 teaspoons ground cumin (reserved)

Nutritional Info
per serving

Calories—226

Carbohydrates—10.5g

Protein—26.75g

Fat—8.25g

Fiber—1g

If you're having friends over on a Friday night, treat them to these wonderful fajitas. Don't be intimidated by the ingredient list, as it cooks quickly and tastes wonderful. This recipe can be used with beef or chicken and does not necessarily need to be served with flour tortillas. You can serve these fajitas with corn tortillas or low-carb tortillas, or with rice to increase the carbohydrate calories. Add the meat to a tasty salad if you're in the mood for something lighter but equally delicious.

Directions

Prepare meat by mixing all marinade ingredients except lime juice, cornstarch and cumin together in a small bowl. Marinate beef in a glass bowl or container, preferably overnight, stirring a few times to ensure even marinating. Reserve the lime juice, cumin and cornstarch for use just prior to cooking the fajitas.

To cook meat, heat a half-tablespoon oil in a wok or large skillet over high heat. Cook meat until it has browned; remove from wok and set aside. Heat remaining half-tablespoon of oil in wok, add onions, garlic and bell peppers into the wok and cook until onions are soft. Stir in the remaining marinade ingredients (cumin, lime juice and cornstarch). This will form a light sauce for the vegetables. Combine meat and tomatoes with vegetables and cook until hot. Squeeze fresh lemon or lime over meat just before serving with your chosen sidedishes.

Suggested garnishes: lime wedges, jalapenos, guacamole (page 165), salsa (page 163), fat-free sour cream or pico de gallo (page 157).

Red and Green Pepper Steak

This colorful and lean stir-fry will allow you to enjoy the taste of fresh meat and vegetables without drenching them in heavy gravy. You can use green, red, yellow or orange bell peppers or a nice combination of them if you want to give this a dressed-up taste and appearance. Serve over a salad or brown rice.

Directions

Preheat wok or skillet and sauté garlic in half-tablespoon of the soy for one minute. Add beef and cook until meat has almost reached your desired level of doneness. Add vegetables and cook until vegetables have softened. Season with pepper and remaining soy.

Modifications

Try adding water chestnuts, bean sprouts, red pepper flakes, fresh tomatoes or fresh jalapeno to this dish to see how you like it.

4 servings

Ingredients

1 pound top round or flank steak (cut in strips or small pieces)

1 large green pepper, sliced

1 medium red pepper, sliced

1 medium yellow onion, chopped

1 teaspoon minced garlic (3 cloves)

1 tablespoon reduced-sodium soy sauce, reduced-sodium beef broth or liquid aminos

Fresh ground pepper, to taste

Nutritional Info
per serving

Calories—133.75

Carbohydrates—5.25g

Protein—25g

Fat—3.75g

Fiber—.75g

Beef and Broccoli

4 servings

Ingredients

1 pound top round or flank steak
   (cut in strips or small pieces)

4 cups broccoli, cut
   (2 medium heads)

½ medium yellow onion, chopped

2 teaspoons minced garlic (6 cloves)

¼ cup reduced-sodium beef broth

Fresh ground pepper, to taste

Anyone for a dose of protein, fiber and vitamin C? This lean version of beef and broccoli will keep you feeling full and satisfied due to its fiber count. It's not fried in oil either, so even if you're watching your calorie intake carefully, you can still enjoy this dish.

Directions

Preheat wok or skillet and sauté garlic in one tablespoon of the broth for one minute. Add beef and cook until meat has almost reached your desired level of doneness. Add onions, broccoli and remaining beef broth and cook until vegetables have softened. Note that covering the pan with a lid for a few minutes will allow the broccoli to steam better and accelerate the cooking time of this last step. Serve over brown rice.

Nutritional Info
per serving

Calories—151

Carbohydrates—6.25g

Protein—28g

Fat—4.25g

Fiber—2.64g

Lightening Fast Fajitas

Fajitas as served in a restaurant are usually a great treat. This is a cheat version of fajitas to make when you don't have time to prepare traditional fajitas.

Directions

Sauté garlic in a bit of lemon juice for one minute in large wok or skillet. Add beef and chili powder and cook until beef is nearly the temperature you desire. Add peppers and onions and cook until vegetables are soft. Raise the heat for a short time toward the end of cooking if you like the vegetables slightly charred. Top with salsa or fat-free sour cream if desired. Serve over rice or salad.

4 servings

Ingredients

1 pound flank steak
(cut in strips or small pieces)

1 large green pepper, cut in strips

1 red pepper, cut in strips

1 medium yellow onion, cut in strips

3 cloves pressed garlic

1 teaspoon chili powder

Lemon juice

Fresh ground pepper to taste

Nutritional Info
per serving

Calories—139.5

Carbohydrates—7g

Protein— 25g

Fat— 3.75g

Fiber—1.4g

Ingredients

1 pound 96% extra lean ground beef

¼ cup onion, diced

½ large green pepper, diced

2 egg whites, beaten

¼ cup oat bran or oatmeal
(quick or old fashioned)

½ teaspoon garlic powder

8 ounces reduced-sodium
tomato sauce

Pepper to taste

Nutritional Info
per serving

Calories—172

Carbohydrates—9g

Protein— 23.5g

Fat—5g

Fiber—1.78g

Laree's
Fit and Lean Meatloaf

Meatloaf always makes a quick family dinner, and you don't need the whole eggs or breadcrumbs of the traditional version to make an outstanding dish. In fact, by using oatmeal, you'll be adding a little fiber as you contribute to the flavor and texture of the meat.

Directions

Preheat oven 350 degrees. Mix meat, vegetables, eggs, garlic powder, oatbran (or oatmeal), and half of the tomato sauce together in medium-sized bowl. Spoon mixture into an 8x8 square baking pan or bread loaf pan sprayed with nonstick cooking spray. Top loaf with remaining tomato sauce and bake for approximately 50 minutes. Makes 4 large slices.

Stuffed Peppers

These quick-cooking stuffed peppers are bulked with nutritious brown rice instead of breadcrumbs. Try making a batch of them using red, yellow and green peppers for more variety.

Directions

Preheat oven to 350 degrees. Begin preparation by cooking rice according to package directions. Brown rice takes about 40 minutes to cook, so if you are short on time, use instant brown rice for this recipe. Slice the tops off the green peppers and remove the seeds. Boil the green peppers in a saucepan for five minutes and set them aside. Cook ground beef and onions in a non-stick skillet until browned. Stir in cooked rice, diced tomatoes and spices. Place peppers in an un-greased baking dish and fill each with an equal amount of the beef and rice mixture. Cover dish with lid or aluminum foil and bake for 30 minutes.

Modifications

Shortcut, lower-carb version: You can omit the rice and stewed tomatoes from this recipe if you wish to save preparation time or shave off unwanted carbohydrates. Follow the instructions to this recipe, but replace the filling with the Lean Meatloaf mixture from page 24. Bake at 350 degrees for about 50 minutes.

IN STELLA'S KITCHEN

Brown Rice Blues? Do you avoid cooking brown rice because it takes too long to cook? If so, make a giant batch on a quiet Sunday afternoon while you relax or do chores. Once cooked, measure single-portions into plastic baggies for freezing. Later, you can thaw a portion of the pre-cooked rice in the microwave for a sidedish or to add to a recipe.

4 servings

Ingredients

4 large green peppers

1 pound 96% extra lean ground beef

½ cup yellow onion, diced

1 14-ounce can reduced-sodium stewed tomatoes

1 cup brown rice, cooked

½ teaspoon garlic powder

1 teaspoon dried basil

Nutritional Info
per serving

Calories—270

Carbohydrates—31.25g

Protein—26.5g

Fat—5.5g

Fiber—1.61g

What's in a Name?

Have you ever walked to the meat aisle of a grocery story intent on finding a particular cut of meat only to find they were out? Chances are—at least if you weren't born in Texas—this has happened at least once in your life simply because you didn't know the various names for the same piece of meat. In fact, you've probably passed up a great sale not realizing a sale package of meat was cut from the same part of the animal as the original cut you were planning to use. This butcher's block tip sheet will help you decipher beef cuts you purchase, and might even save you money.

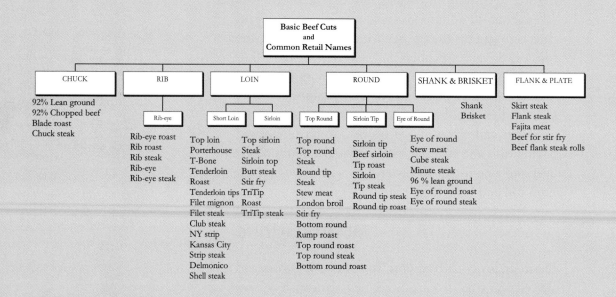

2 Success Tips for Cooking Delicious Beef

Sear meat—Browning meat quickly over high heat before the inside is cooked will help seal the meat so that flavor is locked in. You should sear meat prior to any cooking method such as stewing, roasting or braising.

Rest meat—Allowing meat to rest five to six minutes per pound before serving will give the natural juices time to spread throughout the meat. This will result in more tender, succulent meat. For thinner steaks, the time it generally takes to prepare the remainder of the plate allows sufficient rest time.

Seared New York Strip Steaks with Basil and Wine

4 servings

This is an impressive display for even the most helpless cook. The basil and white wine create a simple glaze that will add an interesting flair to your steak. This recipe calls for white wine, but will taste great if all you've got on hand is red. You can also substitute the basil with fresh rosemary.

Ingredients

1 pound New York strip steaks

4 cloves garlic, finely diced

1½ cup white wine

5 basil leaves, fresh, chopped

½ teaspoon light olive oil

¾ cup warm water (to deglaze pan)

Fresh ground pepper to taste

Directions

Moisten the bottom of a heavy skillet with light olive oil; cook garlic over medium heat until it begins to brown. Raise the temperature to high and sear both sides of steaks. Add the basil and the wine, a half-cup at a time, allowing the wine to "reduce" completely before adding more wine. A reduction time of approximately seven minutes will yield medium rare steaks. Lower the heat slightly to increase reduction time if you like your steaks cooked to a higher temperature. Once steaks are cooked to desired doneness, place them on a warm serving plate and deglaze the skillet using ¾ cup of warm water. This will produce a very thin sauce to pour over the steaks.

IN STELLA'S KITCHEN

Deducing Reducing—The culinary technique of reducing a liquid (broth, sauce or wine) entails allowing it to boil at a high temperature and evaporate. This results in a thicker, more intensely flavored sauce called a "reduction" used to glaze the final masterpiece.

Nutritional Info
per serving

Calories—200

Carbohydrates—1g

Protein—29g

Fat—6g

Fiber—trace

Ingredients

1 pound top round or flank steak,
  cubed or cut across grain into strips

1½ tablespoon reduced-sodium
  teriyaki marinade

2 tablespoons arrowroot

1½ teaspoon crushed garlic (3 cloves)

1 tablespoon safflower oil
  (high oleic if you can find it)

1 red bell pepper, cubed

1 green bell pepper, cubed

¼ cup green onions, chopped

1 teaspoon red pepper flakes
  (omit if you don't like spicy teriyaki)

1 teaspoon sesame seeds (optional)

Nutritional Info
per serving

Calories—149.75

Carbohydrates—5.5g

Protein—25g

Fat—5.25g

Fiber—trace

Spicy Beef
and Vegetable Teriyaki

Here's a quick version of Chinese take-out that gives you full control over the sodium and fat used to prepare the food. Not only does it taste great, but it takes only 30 minutes to make and costs a fraction of the restaurant versions. You do not need to follow the traditional method of frying the vegetables in oil as the natural juices of the vegetables will be released while they cook and prevent them from sticking to the pan.

Directions

Combine teriyaki marinade, safflower oil, arrowroot and garlic in a small bowl and marinate meat in mixture for about 20 minutes. While the meat is marinating, cut the vegetables and prepare rice or salad to serve with the teriyaki if desired. In a large, nonstick skillet or wok sprayed with nonstick cooking spray, sauté the bell peppers and green onions for about three minutes and remove from heat. Next, pour meat and marinade into wok and stir-fry meat for about three minutes. (There's no need for additional oil as there is already some in the marinade.) Add vegetables back to the mixture and stir-fry until hot. Sprinkle with sesame seeds if desired.

IN STELLA'S KITCHEN

Quick marinating—While it's nice to plan ahead so that you can marinate your stir-fry meat, it's just not always possible. However, even just a quick 10- to 20-minute marinade can make a difference. To find the 20 minutes, just re-arrange some of your cooking steps. Instead of cooking the meat first, allow it to marinate while you cut and cook vegetables and get sidedishes going or perhaps even set the table. You only need a few minutes to cook the meat and you'll be able to serve it fresh from the wok.

Low-Fat Stuffed Manicotti with Roasted Red Pepper Sauce

One of the most useful kitchen tools you can have is a palate with a sense of adventure and an occasional taste for experimentation. Such kitchen fun will keep you amused while you appreciate wholesome food. Most versions of manicotti served in Italian restaurants are drenched in sauce and too much cheese. Deviate from that and try this interesting low-fat and delicious manicotti made with herbed chevre—a soft French cheese made from goat milk.

Directions

Preheat oven to 450 degrees. Boil shells according to package directions and set aside. If you are using fresh red peppers, roast them in a nonstick skillet over medium-high heat, turning them so each side of the pepper is charred. Place peppers in plastic bag until the steam loosens the skin from the pepper flesh. Peel off skins, remove seeds and stems and puree in blender with olive oil, a quarter-teaspoon of the ground pepper and basil. Set aside.

For the filling, warm a nonstick skillet over medium heat and spray with nonstick cooking spray. Sauté ground beef and onions until beef is no longer pink and onions are soft. Add garlic and cook just long enough for it to release its aroma (30–45 seconds). Remove mixture from heat and transfer to medium-sized mixing bowl. Add remaining ingredients and mix everything together. Stuff pasta shells with filling and place in 8x8 baking dish sprayed with nonstick cooking spray. Pour sauce on shells and over edges of shells so they don't dry out while cooking. Bake shells until sauce bubbles (about 25 minutes). Sprinkle with freshly grated Parmesan if desired.

Ingredients

6 manicotti shells

3 red bell peppers
(or 10-ounce jar roasted red peppers)

¾ pound 96% extra lean ground beef

½ teaspoon ground black pepper

½ teaspoon basil

1 teaspoon crushed garlic

½ small onion

2 ounces herbed chevre
(herbed goat cheese)

1 large egg white, beaten

½ cup fat-free cottage cheese
(or fat-free ricotta)

Nutritional Info
per filled shell

Calories—200

Carbohydrates—19.9g

Protein—19.5g

Fat—4.8g

Fiber—2.3g

The Basics of Cooking Lean with Beef

There's more to eating lean with beef than simply selecting the right cut of meat. Try some of these tried and true methods for reducing the amount of added fat and calories in prepared beef dishes.

Braise

Braising produces very tender beef, similar to making a stew except only the bottom third of the meat rests in liquid. The remainder of the meat cooks by steam from the simmering liquid. Remaining liquid from cooking a braised dish (such as Yankee Pot Roast) can be used to make a sauce to drizzle over the meat.

To braise beef: Brown meat at a high temperature, place it in a roasting pan filled one third to one half with water and vegetables, and cook at 300° until the meat pulls apart (about three hours).

Suggested cuts: top round, eye of round, sirloin tip round roast, flank steak

Stew

Stewing is a method of cooking beef by immersing it completely in liquid. The liquid becomes the "soup." Unlike a roast, stew meat should be cut into small chunks before cooking.

To stew beef: Cut beef into cubes and brown it at high heat in a very tiny amount of light olive oil. Some like to dust it in flour but this is not necessary. Add meat and vegetables to a large soup pot and cover half-way with water. The remaining liquid can be broth, canned tomatoes, wine or a combination of all three. Simmer (not boil) until beef is cooked and vegetables are soft, or cook in a crockpot set to low while you are out for the day. Add dry herbs during the last hour of cooking.

Suggested cuts: top round roast, eye of round roast, sirloin tip round roast

Roast

Roasting beef entails cooking a whole slab of beef "dry" in the oven.

To roast beef: Put the meat on a rack inside a roasting pan to ensure it cooks evenly. The meat should be basted occasionally with broth or its own juices—basting with plain water will dry it out. Cooking times will vary according to how well done you prefer the meat, and if you've used specially labeled "lean" or "light" beef (which take a third less time to cook than regular shelf meats—see time chart on page 19). Use a meat thermometer for accuracy and follow the instructions in the recipes for best results.

Suggested cuts: top round roast, rump roast (sirloin top butt roast), rib or rib-eye roast, tenderloin roast

Grill

Grilling is done by cooking of beef over open flame or an intense heat source. Often meat is rubbed with spices or marinades before grilling. Grilling steaks should be one to one-and-a-half inches thick and filets up to two inches thick.

To grill beef: If you are grilling outdoors, your charcoal coals should be ash gray and you should only be able to hold your hand over the grill for three to four seconds. The thickest pieces of meats should be placed at the coolest section of the grill because they will need longer to cook and you don't want to burn them.

Suggested cuts: rib-eye steak, 92–96% extra lean ground beef, flank steak, steak tenderloin, tenderloin filet, New York strip, London broil, sirloin steak/top butt

Broil

Broiled meat is a super-fast and very hot method of cooking at very hot temperatures. Watch your meat closely as you learn the technique of broiling.

To broil beef: Set rack three to four inches from top heat coils for meats up to one-and-a-half inches thick and four to five inches away for cuts up to two-and-a-half inches thick. Set oven temperature to broil (500 degrees). Meat should be placed on a rack and turned when the top side has browned. It will take less time for the second side to brown.

Suggested cuts: New York strip, rib-eye steak, London broil, sirloin steak/top butt, steak tenderloin

Stir fry

Stir-fried meats are typically cooked in oil, but oil is not necessary. All you really need is a little moisture to prevent the meat from sticking until it is cooked.

To stir fry: Use a nonstick wok or pan sprayed with nonstick cooking spray and use the natural fat of the meat, apple juice, liquid aminos or vegetable stock to cook meat. Add vegetables after meat has cooked, or cook seperately to save preparation time.

Suggested cuts: flank steak (most popular), tenderloin, rib-eye steak, top or eye of round (cut thinly), round strip steak, sirloin top butt

Brick House Beef Kabobs

Here's a delicious way of eating the protein blocks necessary for building muscle. These kabobs can be grilled on an indoor electric grill too. Be sure to turn them so all sides are cooked evenly.

Directions

Mx marinade ingredients in glass bowl well; set aside. Prick meat chunks with fork and soak in marinade overnight if possible. Place alternating pieces of meat and vegetables on the skewer sticks. Grill to desired temperature and serve.

Modifications

Pineapple chunks, cherry tomatoes, eggplant, corn or squash are also terrific vegetables to skewer onto kabobs.

4 servings

Ingredients

1 pound top round, cut in 1" cubes

1 large onion, cut in chunks

1 small red bell pepper, cubed

1 small green bell pepper, cubed

8 whole mushrooms

4-8 skewers
(soak wooden skewers overnight)

Marinade
½ cup reduced-sodium soy sauce

1 tablespoon white wine
or red wine vinegar

½ teaspoon ground ginger

3 cloves of garlic finely chopped

3 ounces light beer

1 tablespoon onion powder

Nutritional Info
per serving

Calories—183

Carbohydrates—11g

Protein—27.1g

Fat— 3.4g

Fiber—2.5g

Wisconsin Pot Roast Packets

4 servings

These meat and potato packets are similar in taste to a pot roast but much more convenient. These pot roast packets are easily prepared by those with limited kitchen skills.

Directions

Preheat oven to 350 degrees. Lay out large pieces of aluminum foil and place equal amount of all ingredients on one side of foil. Fold foil inward at all seams to form a packet, allowing foil to tent slightly on top to allow room for steam. Pinch all edges closed. You do not need to add liquid. Bake packets on cookie sheet or in shallow baking dish for 45 minutes.

IN STELLA'S KITCHEN

Packet purchases—You can purchase foil packets in several sizes at the grocery store for use in packet meals of all sizes. Try using them for chicken and shrimp dishes, or for mixed vegetable sidedishes, too.

Ingredients

1 pound top round cut into 1″ cubes

1 large baking potato (or sweet potato), cut into chunks

1 medium yellow onion, chopped

1 green bell pepper, sliced into rings

¾ cup sliced carrots

Seasoning of choice (salt-free steak seasoning or salt and pepper)

Nutritional Info
per serving

Calories—250

Carbohydrates—27.4g

Protein—27.7g

Fat—3.3g

Fiber—3.9g

33

Ingredients

1 pound 96% extra lean ground beef

½ cup yellow onion, chopped

¾ tablespoon chili powder

¼ teaspoon ground cumin

½ teaspoon garlic powder

½ teaspoon red pepper flakes (optional)

Dash of oregano

1 14-ounce can reduced-sodium diced tomatoes, undrained

½ cup frozen or canned corn kernels, drained (optional)

1 14-ounce can chopped green chilies, drained or ½ cup green pepper, diced

8 cup shredded romaine, green leaf or red leaf lettuce (12 leaves)

Nutritional Info
per serving

Calories—215

Carbohydrates—15.8g

Protein—26.3g

Fat—5.2g

Fiber-2.8g

Oly's Beef Taco Salad

Not everyone in my family was born in the kitchen. The first year or two into my sister's marriage, her family survived on her taco salads while she honed her culinary techniques. This modified version suses leafy greens instead of tortilla chips or deep-fried tortilla bowls.

Directions

Cook ground beef and onion in a large nonstick skillet over medium heat until beef is no longer pink. Drain. Stir in tomatoes, corn and seasonings and bring to a boil. Reduce heat and simmer for about 10 minutes, stirring occasionally. Serve meat mixture over greens and sprinkle with choice of optional garnishes.

Modifications

Try using diced tomatoes, reduced-fat cheese, salsa (see page 163), nonfat sour cream or a minimal amount of crushed, baked tortilla chips as a garnish on top of the salad.

Beefy Montana Stew

One of the first people to indulge my kitchen curiosities was a kindly next-door neighbor originally from Victor, Montana. She had a whole bookshelf of well-worn cookbooks and the patience to show a neighborhood kid how to make molasses cookies or explain useful ingredients and herbs. This is just the kind of wholesome stew I can imagine smelling under the big, blue-sky country in the background of the family photos of her home.

Directions

Heat a large soup pot over medium-high heat and spray with nonstick cooking spray. Brown beef evenly. Add onion and garlic and cook until onions are soft. Add remaining ingredients and bring to a boil. Reduce heat and simmer until barley is done and carrots are soft.

Modifications

You can substitute browned extra lean ground beef in place of stew meat if you are short on time.

This can be cooked in a crockpot set to low for the day.

Add chopped spinach to stew, or replace the barley with wild rice or brown rice

12 servings

Ingredients

2 pounds top round or eye or round, cut into 1 or 2″ cubes

1 14-ounce can reduced-sodium tomato sauce

1 14-ounce can reduced-sodium crushed tomatoes

2 cups reduced-sodium beef broth

½ cup pearled barley (uncooked)

½ medium onion, chopped

1 cup chopped celery

¾ cup sliced carrots

1½ teaspoon minced garlic

¼ teaspoon black pepper

½ teaspoon parsley

1 crushed bay leaf

1½ cup water

Nutritional Info
per serving

Calories—166

Carbohydrates—15.2g

Protein—19.2g

Fat—3.2g

Fiber—2.8g

Ingredients

2 pounds top round
 (or other roasting cut)

1½ teaspoon crushed garlic

2 pounds new potatoes, cut in half

1 large onion, sliced

1 cup baby carrots (or sliced carrots)

½ cup celery, sliced

1 cup green bell pepper, cubed
 (optional)

1 crushed bay leaf

1 cup reduced-sodium beef broth
 (or water)

Salt and pepper

Nutritional Info
per serving

Calories—243

Carbohydrates—25.4g

Protein—28.4g

Fat—3.1g

Fiber—3g

Big Guy's
Homestyle Pot Roast

Here's a hearty and healthy traditional pot roast you can also prepare in a soup pot or crockpot set to low.

Directions

Preheat oven to 400 degrees. Heat a large skillet or sauce-pan over high heat and moisten the bottom with paper towel dampened with a small amount of light olive oil. Sear all sides of roast and remove from heat. Place roast in roasting pan and top with garlic; add salt and pepper. Arrange vegetables around meat and add bay leaf and beef broth. Allow to roast for approximately two hours or until meat is so tender that it almost falls apart.

IN STELLA'S KITCHEN

Spice Rack Fact—When a recipe calls for fresh herbs, you can substitute with dried herbs using a 1 to 3 ratio. Use one teaspoon dried herb for every tablespoon of fresh herbs.

Captain Nielson's Viking Stew

Here's a hearty stew for "meat and potato" guys (or gals!) inspired by the brawny Nordic men who once traveled the high seas.

Directions

Moisten bottom of large soup pot with a tiny bit of light olive oil. Sear meat chunks over high heat, then reduce heat to medium. Add all remaining ingredients and bring to a boil. Reduce heat to low and allow to simmer about one hour or until meat is tender and potatoes and carrots are soft, adding warm water to reach desired stock consistency. This stew can also cook in a crockpot set on low for eight hours or more.

IN STELLA'S KITCHEN

Herbology—When cooking with fresh herbs, always add them in the last few minutes of cooking.

10 servings

Ingredients

2 pounds top round, cut in cubes

1 cup onions, sliced

1 cup red wine

2 8-ounce cans reduced-sodium tomato sauce

1 28-ounce can whole or crushed tomatoes

2 teaspoon garlic, crushed

1 tablespoon Worcestershire sauce

2 pounds new potatoes, cut in half (or cut up baking potatoes)

1½ cup celery, sliced (5-6 stalks)

1 cup reduced-sodium, fat-free beef broth

¾ cup baby carrots or sliced carrots

1 tablespoon dried basil

Salt and pepper to taste

Nutritional Info
per serving

Calories—236

Carbohydrates—28.58g

Protein—24.2g

Fat—2.8g

Fiber—3.8g

37

Butcher Basics

There are so many cuts and brands of beef it's hard to tell which are the smart cuts to buy. There are multiple names and descriptive labels for the same cuts that confuse even the most well-meaning consumer—so much that they do not know which meats are leaner or of better quality. Here are a few guidelines to help you understand the basic principles of buying beef.

Don't be misled by tricky labeling

Prime, Choice and Select grades of beef are indicative of a cut's leanness, palatability and the age of the animal. Select cuts are leaner than choice cuts, and choice cuts are leaner than prime cuts. Select cuts will appear less marbled when compared with a prime cut and will not be as tender or juicy as choice or prime cuts that have a higher marbled fat content. Prime grades are aged and generally sold in fine restaurants or specialty meat shops. Select and choice grades can be found in the grocery store and other restaurants, but keep in mind that select cuts are the leanest. You can work around any tenderness concerns over using lean beef with marinades and a little know-how of properly cooking beef.

Selecting cuts and brands

One of the easiest ways to choose leaner cuts is to look for special labeling on the packages. Look for the American Heart Association's heart healthy logo or a "USDA lite" or "USDA light" sticker on the packaging. Most often, these choices are special brands from cattle farms that specialize in producing leaner "natural," "free-range," or "hormone-free" beef. Examples of some national "light" brands are: Laura's Lean Beef, Naturalite, and some Cattleman's Collection special cuts. This type of beef is even leaner, lower in calories, and lower in fat than regular brands and is the kind of beef used to calculate the nutritional values in these recipes. The American Heart Association Guidelines define extra lean beef as a 4-ounce serving which contains: five grams total fat or less, with two grams or less coming from saturated fat and less than 95 milligrams cholesterol.

Where does the beef you buy appear on the graphic on the next page?

Fat Content and Caloric Value Comparison
for 4-ounce Beef Portions

Low Fat			High Fat		
3g fat 120 cals	5g fat 145 cals	9g fat 160 cals	20g fat 280 cals		Dietary Doom
Top round	Eye of round 96% lean Ground beef	Sirloin top butt Beef flank steak Tenderloin filet	92% lean Ground beef Rib-eye	73% lean Ground beef	Prime rib (up to 30g)

Color

Extra lean meat is packed tighter than regular ground beef and is typically kept on the butcher block for a shorter period of time than regular meat. Extra lean beef is typically a brighter red in appearance and less marbled. Extra lean ground beef is a darker brown or purplish in the center due to the lack of oxygen. When open and exposed to air, it will turn bright red.

Beef on a budget

Since extra lean beef is a higher quality, it is sold to consumers at a premium price; many cost-conscious people avoid purchasing lean cuts of beef. Here are a few ways you can afford to include beef in your menu.

- √ Remember, you are not paying for fatty marbling, but pure beef you can eat instead of discarding.

- √ Make it a rule to never buy meat except when it's on sale.

- √ Every grocery chain will have weekly meat sales to draw people into the store—watch the ad circulars for sales.

- √ Talk to the butcher and ask what cuts will be on sale the following week.

- √ You should also ask what time they mark down the day's meat. Shopping at that time can yield savings of over 50%.

- √ Freeze what you won't be using right away to reduce waste.

4 servings

Ingredients

1 pound eye of round steak

1 teaspoon olive oil

2 ½ teaspoons fresh ground pepper (ground coarsely)

½ teaspoon salt

½ cup reduced-sodium beef broth

½ cup Cabernet Sauvignon wine

3 tablespoons sugar-free or low-sugar raspberry preserves

½ cup fresh or frozen raspberries, chopped roughly (optional)

Nutritional Info
per serving

Calories—181

Carbohydrates—9.2g

Protein—26.6g

Fat—4.7g

Fiber—1g

Pepper-Crusted Eye of Round with Raspberry Cabernet Glaze

Eye of round is one of the leanest cuts of beef available. This simple glaze brings a lot of character to the meat that you might expect in a more marbled cut. While the recipe sounds a little on the gourmet side, the raspberry cabernet glaze is actually very easy to make. From start to finish, this shouldn't take any longer than 20–25 minutes to prepare, cook and serve.

Directions

Combine pepper and salt and spread evenly on a dinner plate or other flat, clean surface. Rub sides of steaks with olive oil and press both sides onto plate to pepper-crust steaks. Heat a nonstick skillet over medium-high heat and spray with nonstick cooking spray. Cook steaks to desired temperature and remove from pan. Turn heat to high and add wine, broth and preserves to pan. Bring to a boil and add fresh raspberries. Allow sauce to reduce by half, then drizzle over steaks.

Modifications

Depending on the preserves that are used, cooks may find the carmelization that occurs when preparing a sugar-free glaze is a little different than a traditional glaze. The natural fructose of the fresh raspberries will help overcome this difference enough for most palates. If not, a small amount of brown sugar (a teaspoon or so) can be used.

Giovanni's Quick Big Beef Lasagna

Making a big, hefty lasagna can sometimes be a treat, but it's intimidating for some, or unrealistic for small families and single people. This smaller 8x8 lasagna has been modified so that it is not only quick and easy to make, but higher in protein and lower in fat and carbohydrates than traditional lasagna. Leftover slices can be easily frozen for a healthy, preservative-free frozen dinner.

Directions

Preheat oven to 375 degrees. Spray a nonstick skillet with cooking spray and cook ground beef over medium heat until meat is brown. Drain. Return to heat, add onions and garlic and cook for an additional minute. Remove from heat and set aside. Mix all remaining ingredients except sauce and cheese together in a large mixing bowl. Stir in cooked beef crumbles. Spray bottom of an 8x8 baking dish with nonstick spray and spoon in a few tablespoons of sauce to coat bottom of pan. Lay two lasagna noodles into the baking disch and top with a few more tablespoons of the sauce. Spoon half of the filling mixture onto the noodles. Repeat process (you will have two layers of filling). Cover final layer of lasagna noodles with remaining sauce and top with cheese. Bake covered with foil for about 30 minutes or until sauce is bubbling. Remove foil and continue to bake until cheese is lightly browned. Allow lasagna to rest a few minutes before cutting.

Modifications

Mushrooms, eggplant, green pepper, basil and any other vegetables of choice can be added into each layer.

6 servings

Ingredients

6 pieces oven-ready, no-boil lasagna noodles

1 pound 96% extra lean ground beef

½ cup yellow onion, diced

1 teaspoon crushed garlic

1½ cup low-fat ricotta cheese

1 cup low-fat cottage cheese

3 egg whites, beaten

1 teaspoon basil

1 teaspoon oregano

1 teaspoon fresh ground pepper

¾ cup reduced-fat Mozzarella cheese (made from skim milk)

Quick Fresh Tomato Sauce on page 155, or one 16-ounce can of reduced-sodium, low-fat prepared sauce

Nutritional Info
per serving

Calories—313

Carbohydrates—22.6g

Protein—32g

Fat—10.6g

Fiber—.9g

Ingredients

2 pounds 96% extra lean
   ground beef or ground buffalo

½ bag (1½ cup) Ham's brand
   15-Bean Soup Mix
   (discard seasoning packet)

1 14-ounce reduced-sodium
   stewed diced tomatoes

1 6-ounce can no-salt added
   tomato paste

1 cup yellow onion, diced

¼ cup Red Hot brand seasoning
   or Tabasco sauce

½ cup celery, chopped

4 cloves garlic

1 small can green chilies, drained

1 cup green bell pepper, diced

2 jalapeno peppers, seeded and
   de-veined, finely diced (optional)

½ tablespoon chili powder

1½ teaspoon ground cumin

1 teaspoon oregano

1 teaspoon parsley

Fresh ground pepper, salt substitute
   or other dry seasonings of choice

Nutritional Info
per serving

Calories—270

Carbohydrates—28.3g

Protein—27.4g

Fat—5.2g

Fiber—9.4g

Wild Bill's
15-Bean Texas Chili

Round up the posse for some football and steamin' hot 5-alarm Texas chili that's high in fiber—over nine grams per serving. This chili is a meal in itself with an exceptional protein count and a rich blend of complex carbohydrates. There's no substituting the flavor of fresh cooked beans in this recipe so be sure to prepare them the night before the big game.

Directions

Rinse a half-package of Ham's beans under cool water and discard any broken beans. Place beans in a 2½ quart heavy saucepan or crockpot and fill pan within an inch of the top with water. Add one teaspoon of salt. Bring beans to a boil and then reduce heat to the lowest heat setting and simmer overnight. In the morning, remove cooked beans from heat and refrigerate until ready to prepare chili. In large soup pot, cook ground beef over medium heat until beef is no longer pink. Drain the excess oils, add onions, peppers and garlic to beef and cook until vegetables are slightly softened and beef is browned. Transfer beans to soup pot mixture and add all remaining ingredients. Bring to a boil, reduce heat and cover with lid. Allow to simmer at least 35 minutes over low heat. When simmering longer than 35 minutes, stir occasionally and check water levels, adding more water if mixture is too thin or allowing water to steam off for a thicker consistency. Serve alone or with nonfat sour cream, reduced-fat cheese or diced onions.

Proper Beef Storage

Did you know that when left at room temperature, the bacteria in beef doubles every 20 minutes? For optimal taste and freshness, finish your other grocery shopping before selecting your meat purchases. When you get home, cut your beef into useable portions, re-wrap it tightly in a freezer bag, aluminum foil or freezer paper if it will not be used within two weeks. Refrigerate or freeze it as soon as possible. Storage times for beef vary according to how much the beef has been processed.

Refrigerator storage times

Ground beef: 1–2 days. Ground meat has the largest percentage of meat surface exposed to air due to the grinding process and therefore has a shorter storage time.

Stew meat, kabob meat, and stir-fry meat: 2–3 days. Since stew meat is cut into smaller pieces, a greater surface area is exposed to air. While these cuts have a longer refrigerator storage time when compared to ground beef, they still have a shorter shelf life than large whole muscle cuts.

Steaks and roasts: 3–4 days. Whole muscle cuts have a limited amount of meat surface exposed to air and therefore keep longer in the refrigerator.

Freezer storage times
Frozen at 0°F or colder, re-wrapped prior to freezing

Ground beef: 3–4 months

Stew meat, kabob meat and stir-fry meat: 6–12 months

Steaks and roasts: 6–12 months

Defrosting

Never leave meat on the counter to defrost or marinate. Defrost meat in the refrigerator overnight. It should remain refrigerated until just before cooking.

Source: 2002 National Cattlemen's Beef Association

2
Poultry

Chicken, turkey and other poultry are extremely versatile low-fat proteins that can be found in recipes of almost every culture. In spite of this, many health conscious people wind up consuming chicken breast that's been grilled on a little countertop appliance with a little salt and pepper. Thinking they can't do anything better in the same amount of time, they remain committed to naked chicken day after day. Is there any wonder why so many jump off the health band-wagon almost as quickly as they jumped on? The funny thing is, you can add just about anything you find in your cupboard to a piece of chicken and it will taste good. Spicy, sweet, creamy, baked, boiled, grilled; there's a recipe to match your palate here. Both traditional American and ethnic preparations have been modified to more healthful versions and all of the recipes in this chapter take that same boring piece of chicken breast and give it new pizzazz.

2

Poultry

Quick Curry Chicken

If you like Indian food, you're going to love this easy-to-make curry, and if you haven't tried curry, you're in for a spicy treat. Curry tastes great with brown or fluffy Basmati rice.

Directions

Spray wok with nonstick cooking spray and sauté garlic until lightly browned. Add chicken and cook about halfway through. Add in carrots, celery, peppers and onions. The natural vegetable juices will infuse the chicken nicely while it finishes cooking. When chicken is cooked fully, add remaining ingredients and simmer until ready to serve.

Modifications

Some like it hot—If you like a hotter curry, you can try adding a little Thai red curry paste or adding extra curry powder.

Short on time—Although this tastes best when prepared as suggested, you can make a simple curry by only using green peppers and onions for the vegetables and plain curry powder for the spice.

IN STELLA'S KITCHEN

Crockpot cooking—Any type of stew or meat and vegetable dish can cook easily while you are away. Throw all ingredients in the crockpot and set it to low. If you'll be gone for several hours, your mood will be lightened by the wonderful comforting scent that greets you when you return home.

10 servings

Ingredients

2 ½ pounds boneless, skinless chicken breast, cut in chunks

1 can 14-ounce, reduced-sodium stewed tomatoes

1 medium yellow onion, chopped

1 carrot, peeled, sliced

1 stalk celery, chopped

1 medium squash, peeled, chopped

3 cloves garlic, peeled, chopped

1 large green pepper, chopped

1 bunch fresh spinach, washed, dried

1 chicken bullion cube

1 tablespoon curry powder

½ teaspoon each: turmeric, coriander, cumin, ginger

Nutritional Info
per serving

Calories—153

Carbohydrates—7.3g

Protein—27.5g

Fat—1.6g

Fiber—2g

47

Ingredients

- 3 pounds boneless, skinless chicken breast halves
- 4 tablespoons New Mexico Chile powder
- 1 cup canned, dried or jarred chipotle chile peppers (if you can find them; these are optional)
- 2 tablespoons 100% whole wheat flour or oat flour
- 3 cloves crushed garlic
- 1 teaspoon dried oregano
- ½ teaspoon ground cumin
- 2 cups warm water

Nutritional Info
per serving

Calories—133

Carbohydrates—2.3g

Protein—26.7g

Fat—1.8g

Fiber—1g

Sedona Chicken Grill

The color of this low-fat, low-carb alternative to carne adovada reminds me of the sun setting over the red rock formations in beautiful Sedona, Arizona. This fairly mild chile dish is best served with steamed rice or black beans and fresh lime wedges.

Directions

Spray a large nonstick skillet with cooking spray. Toast flour by sautéing it in the pan until hot. Add chile powder and stir until blended. Slowly stir in water, whisking until all lumps are removed. Stir in spices and chipotle chile peppers and cook over low heat for five minutes. Remove from heat and pour into bowl or shallow baking dish. Add chicken and marinate in refrigerator, overnight if possible. Grill over open flame or on counter-top grilling appliance and reserve marinade if you'd like to pour it over the chicken. If used over finished chicken, marinade should be warmed while the chicken is cooking. This dish can also be baked in the marinade at 325 degrees until the meat is so tender that it pulls apart easily.

IN STELLA'S KITCHEN

Chile facts—The heat of a chile pepper is measured in Scoville heat units ranging from 1–300,000. The tiny habanero pepper is one of about 200 varieties of chile peppers in the world and tips the scale at 300,000 Scovilles; a jalapeno registers at a mere 5,000.

Baked Chicken Parmesan

Here's a much lighter and quicker version of Chicken Parmesan that's baked instead of pan fried. It's great with a side of pasta, but can also be served on a bed of a more complex carbohydrate such as brown rice. Take flavor a step further and steam your brown rice in one-half water, one-half reduced-sodium chicken broth and a half-teaspoon of basil.

Directions

Preheat oven to 375 degrees. Combine all dry ingredients in large bowl and mix well. Dip chicken breasts in egg whites and then coat both sides by dipping them in dry mixture. Spray both sides with nonstick cooking spray; bake chicken in a shallow baking dish for about 30 minutes or until coating is crisp and insides of breasts are no longer pink. During the last five minutes of cooking, warm sauce in microwave or small saucepan. Once the chicken is cooked, top each breast with a quarter-cup of the sauce and a tablespoon of shredded Parmesan cheese.

6 servings

Ingredients

1½ pound boneless, skinless chicken breast halves

2 tablespoons 100% whole-wheat flour (increased to 3 ½ tablespoons if bran is omitted)

¼ cup unprocessed bran flakes (optional)

3 egg whites, beaten

¼ teaspoon fresh ground pepper

½ teaspoon dried Italian herb blend (basil, rosemary, parsley)

¼ teaspoon garlic powder

¼ teaspoon salt

1 cup Quick Fresh Tomato sauce on page 155, or substitute 1 small can reduced-sodium tomato sauce seasoned with 1 teaspoon Italian herbs

4 tablespoons shredded Parmesan cheese

Nutritional Info
per serving

Calories—178

Carbohydrates—6.1g

Protein—29.8g

Fat—3.7g

Fiber—1.3g

Jamaican Jerk Chicken

Ingredients

2 pounds boneless, skinless chicken breasts

1 jalapeno pepper, diced

8 cloves garlic, minced

6 tablespoons fresh lime juice

2 tablespoons fresh grated ginger

1½ tablespoon olive oil

¾ teaspoon allspice

1 teaspoon cinnamon

¾ teaspoon nutmeg

1½ teaspoon fresh ground black pepper

2 packets artificial sweetener

Nutritional Info
per serving

Calories—153

Carbohydrates—2.7g

Protein—26.4g

Fat—4g

Fiber—.3g

The combination of hot and sweet spices lends the tangy zest of the Caribbean to this grilled chicken dish that goes well over a ginger-mint Basmati or brown rice and perhaps a side of energy-packed black beans. The recipe below contains a kitchen cabinet version of jerk seasoning that is lower in sodium than the jerk seasoning you might buy at a grocery store.

Directions

Puree all ingredients except chicken in blender or food processor until smooth. Pour into shallow baking dish or plastic bag and add chicken. You can prepare this up to 24 hours in advance of grilling but let the chicken marinate for a minimum of 30 minutes. Grill chicken, brushing with leftover marinade. You can also heat the remaining marinade and serve it warm over the chicken before serving.

IN STELLA'S KITCHEN

Make the most of special purchases—When making a dish like jerk chicken, try to think of a way to creatively use ingredients you've purchased for the dish but will not be using entirely. In the case of jerk chicken, try grating or slicing some of the ginger and adding it to water or reduced-sodium chicken broth and using it to cook rice. This results in a complementary sidedish and maximizes your purchase and adds flair to the dish.

Zay's
Spicy Chicken Fingers

4 servings

This recipe is included for those of you with children, although you don't need to have children in the house to enjoy it. Here's something you'll feel good about serving your kids—if you've ever looked at the ingredients listed on the box of frozen chicken tenders, you might have been surprised at how many ingredients are necessary to flavor the cheap chicken bits used to make them. You can double or triple the batch and freeze leftovers for later. Try them with the Sugar-Free BBQ Sauce on page 156.

Ingredients

1 pound boneless, skinless chicken breast, cut into strips

3 tablespoons 100% whole-wheat flour (increased to 4 tablespoons if bran is omitted)

2 tablespoons unprocessed bran flakes

2 egg whites, beaten

1 tablespoon Cajun spice mix (optional)

-or-

½ teaspoon fresh ground pepper

1 teaspoon chili powder

¼ teaspoon garlic powder

¼ teaspoon salt

Directions

Preheat oven to 375 degrees. Combine all dry ingredients in large bowl and mix well. Dip chicken pieces in egg whites and then coat both sides by dipping them in dry ingredients. Spray both sides with nonstick cooking spray and bake chicken in a shallow baking dish for about 25 minutes or until coating is crisp and chicken is cooked through.

Nutritional Info
per serving

Calories—152

Carbohydrates—5.7g

Protein—28.6g

Fat—1.6g

Fiber—1.6g

Crispy "Fried" Chicken

Ingredients

2 pounds boneless, skinless chicken breast halves

¼ cup whole-wheat flour

½ cup unprocessed bran flakes (optional)

4 egg whites, beaten

1 teaspoon fresh ground pepper

½ teaspoon garlic powder

1 teaspoon parsley

½ teaspoon salt or salt substitute

This is a healthy alternative to greasy fried chicken. It's still crispy, but baked instead of fried. Unprocessed wheat bran flakes, which are tasteless for the most part, have been added to limit the amount of wheat flour used in this recipe and provide extra crunch. If you normally like a thick coating of batter, you'll still be reasonable safe double-dipping with this recipe.

Directions

Preheat oven to 375 degrees. Combine all dry ingredients in large bowl and mix well. Dip chicken breast halves in egg whites and then coat both sides by dipping them in dry mixture. Dip them again if desired and spray both sides with nonstick cooking spray. Bake chicken in a shallow baking dish for about 30 minutes or until coating is crisp and insides of breasts are no longer pink.

Nutritional Info
per serving

Calories—149

Carbohydrates—5.2g

Protein—28.3g

Fat—1.6g

Fiber—2.1g

Grilled Chicken and Two-Pepper Pasta Salad

This low-fat, full-flavor pasta salad provides a balanced meal in every scoop. It's quick to make and keeps well in the fridge for handy meals. The color combination appeals to the senses more than expensive packaged pasta salad kits. I strongly recommend using fresh basil as it adds a special flavor that's difficult to match with a dried herb.

Directions

While grilling or boiling chicken breast, prepare pasta al dente according to package directions. Drain and rinse pasta in cool water and refrigerate. Chop remaining ingredients. Combine all ingredients in large bowl and chill in covered container until ready to serve.

In Stella's Kitchen

Get stuck? If your pasta is stuck together after draining, rinse it in hot tap water.

8 servings

Ingredients

1 16-ounce package plain rotini, fusilli or penne pasta (not tri-colored)

1 pound boneless, skinless chicken breast chunks (boiled or grilled)

½ cup fat-free Italian dressing (or little olive oil and vinegar to reduce sodium)

1 green bell pepper, chopped

½ red bell pepper, chopped

½ cup chopped onions (optional)

½ cup sliced black olives, drained

6 leaves fresh basil, chopped (or ¾ teaspoon dried)

¼ cup shredded parmesan cheese

Fresh ground pepper to taste

Nutritional Info
per serving

Calories—276

Carbohydrates—36g

Protein—21g

Fat—4.6g

Fiber—2g

Ingredients

1½ pound boneless, skinless
chicken breast

1½ cup fresh mushrooms, sliced

1 can reduced-sodium, low-fat
cream of mushroom soup

½ cup white table wine

¼ cup onions, diced

2 tablespoons fresh parsley
(or 2 teaspoons dried herb)

Nutritional Info
per serving

Calories—159

Carbohydrates—6.4g

Protein—27.8g

Fat—2.4g

Fiber—.6g

Belle's Mushroom Chicken Bake

Baked mushroom chicken displays well over brown rice, but you can also make it into a scrumptious winter soup. Try adding celery, potato, several varieties of mushroom, or some other favorite vegetables to this when you've got the extra time. If you choose soup tonight, thin it with water or nonfat, reduced-sodium chicken broth and simmer it on the stove.

Directions

Preheat over to 350 degrees. Spray a 9x11-inch pan with nonstick cooking spray. Place mushrooms on top of chicken. Mix soup, wine, onions, and parsley together and pour over chicken and mushrooms. Cover with foil and bake for 50 minutes.

IN STELLA'S KITCHEN

No time to cook? At the end of a long day, it can be a challenge to cook something healthy that your family will enjoy. One way around this is to create a small pocket of time by staying up or waking just five minutes from your usual time to "prep" your cooking. When you get home, all you need to do is slip it in the oven to cook.

E-Z Italian Chicken Stew

Nothing beats a hot stew on a cold winter's day. Unfortunately, there's not always time to defrost and sear the beef found in most traditional stews. Here's a 30-minute Italian chicken stew that's so easy to make, you can step around the need to defrost the meat. If you use frozen chicken breast, simply allow for a bit longer cook time so it can defrost while cooking. As the meat cooks, you'll be able to easily pull it apart into bite-sized pieces with a knife or fork and a pair of tongs or move it to a cutting board for cubing.

Directions

Bring tomatoes, bouillon, Italian seasoning and chicken to a boil a large pot. Reduce heat and simmer while preparing remaining vegetables. Add vegetables and simmer until chicken is no longer pink and potatoes and carrots are soft.

IN STELLA'S KITCHEN

Use 'em up—Make the stew with tomatoes that have become too soft to use in a salad.

12 servings

Ingredients

3 pounds boneless, skinless chicken breasts, cubed

1 14-ounce can stewed tomatoes

3 tablespoons Italian seasoning

2 tablespoons powdered, salt-free chicken bouillon (available at health food stores)

1 carrot, peeled, cut in bite-size pieces

1 potato, peeled, cut in bite-size pieces

1 medium zucchini, chopped

1 onion, chopped

2 celery ribs, chopped

Nutritional Info
per serving

Calories—153

Carbohydrates—7.9g

Protein—27.2g

Fat—1.4g

Fiber—1.2g

Chicken Facts

Why do all the recipes in this cookbook only use boneless skinless breast meat?
The breast of the chicken contains the maximum amount of protein per calorie and the least amount of fat compared to the rest of the bird. It is also the easiest piece of the bird to remove the skin, resulting in the largest amount of accessible meat.

Take a look at the nutritional values of 4-ounce portions of various chicken cuts:

Cut	Calories	Fat (g)	Protein (g)
Breast (meat only, skinless)	118	1.4	26.2
Breast (with skin)	188	10.5	23.6
Leg (meat only, skinless)	130	4.3	22.8
Leg (with skin)	206	13.7	20.6
Thigh (meat only, skinless)	129	4.4	22.3
Thigh (with skin)	234	17.3	19.6
Wing (meat only, skinless)	136	4.0	24.9
Wing (with skin)	246	18.1	20.8

Boneless, skinless breast is the most expensive part of the chicken. How can I afford to feed it to my family all the time?

- Buy chicken breast only when it is on sale, and buy as much as your budget will allow. You can get it for 50% off if you shop smartly.

- Remember, you will have less waste when you buy breast meat. Meat is sold by weight, so every ounce of breast you purchase can be used. This does not happen when you buy wings or legs or thighs and throw out skin and bones.

- Don't rely on the chicken to make the meal. A serving for most people is 4–6 ounces; keep this in mind when preparing dishes. Bulk up dishes with vegetables.

- Strive to purchase family packs and "must sell by today" meat. Just be sure to freeze it if you don't plan to use it immediately.

How long does chicken keep? Raw chicken and cooked chicken can be stored in the refrigerator for about two days. Chicken can be frozen for up to one year if wrapped airtight and stored in the coldest part of the freezer.

What are the healthiest methods of preparing chicken? Grilling, baking, broiling and stir-frying in reduced-sodium broth, vegetable or fruit juice are the healthiest ways to prepare chicken.

Why should I make the effort to marinate my chicken? Marinating chicken with any acidic, enzymatic or dairy marinade helps loosen the tough fibers. Marinating from 30–120 minutes is plenty of time to infuse the meat with flavor. Marinating also reduces cooking time and you only need about a half-cup of liquid per pound of meat. You also deserve the culinary experience of well-made food no matter how hectic your life.

Flash Marinate

Flash marinating is a special technique that those challenged by time constraints will appreciate. When you get home from the store, repackage the raw chicken in individual serving sizes in plastic baggies. Toss in spices and other marinade ingredients and freeze. When you take the packages out to thaw, you will simultaneously be allowing the spices and marinades to release flavors and tenderize the chicken. You will not perceive any expense of time, but enjoy a great meal!

Taos Black Bean and Chicken Pockets

4 servings

Ingredients

4 4-ounce boneless,
skinless chicken breasts

2 cups black beans
(retain the juice from the can)

¾ cup salsa
Try the salsa on page 167, or one
small can chopped green chile
peppers, drained.

¼ teaspoon garlic powder

4 tablespoons reduced-fat
mozzarella or Monterey jack
cheese (optional)

These delicious foil packet meals are easy to bake, are high in protein and fiber—a treaty treat brimming with complex carbohydrates for energy.

Directions

Preheat oven to 350 degrees. Mix beans, salsa and garlic powder together and set aside. Center each chicken breast on separate squares of heavy foil (or two sheets of regular household foil). Top each chicken breast with a half-cup of the bean mixture. Wrap each breast in the foil, allowing room in the packet for the ingredients to steam. Bake for approximately 35 minutes. If cheese is desired, open the packets at the end of the cooking time, sprinkle the chicken with the cheese, and seal the packets briefly until the cheese melts.

Nutritional Info
per serving

Calories—271

Carbohydrates—23.3g

Protein—36.8g

Fat—3.5g

Fiber—7.8g

IN STELLA'S KITCHEN

Cooking fresh beens—If you make your own beans, there's a simple way to ensure you use only the highest quality of beens: Dump the raw beans in a pot of water and discard those that rise to the top.

Lean Grilled Chicken and Broccoli Alfredo

A lean version of a popular dish, it's great over rice, pasta or simply eaten alone. If you don't like broccoli, try this with some red and green bell peppers or better yet, some roasted red peppers. You'll add color, flavor and complexity without adding excessive calories or fat to the meal.

Directions

Grill chicken (or just boil if frozen, then cut into chunks) and set aside. While the chicken is cooking, prepare the sauce. Add broccoli or other vegetables to the sauce. Spoon sauce over the cooked chicken breasts or stir chicken chunks into the sauce. Serve over brown rice or pasta.

IN STELLA'S KITCHEN

Always on the go? The key to surviving a healthy-eating crisis is preparation. When you make any type of sauce for a dish, make a double batch while you've got the ingredients on hand. Freeze the extra sauce for a day when you're short on time.

6 servings

Ingredients

1½ pounds chicken breast, cooked and cut in chunks

2 cups cut broccoli

Low-fat Alfredo Sauce (see page 159)

Nutritional Info
per serving

Calories—222
Carbohydrates—5.4g
Protein—39.2g
Fat—4.8g
Fiber—.9g

Fast Chicken Fajita Salad

1 serving

Ingredients

4 ounces boneless, skinless breast

¼ cup onion, sliced

½ cup green pepper, sliced

3 cups dark leafy greens, washed
and torn into bite-size pieces

2 tablespoons salsa

½ tablespoon reduced-sodium soy,
liquid aminos or lemon juice

1 tablespoon fat-free sour cream
(optional)

Nutritional Info
per serving

Calories—206

Carbohydrates—13.6g

Protein—29.4g

Fat—3.8g

Fiber—3.9g

There are two kinds of fajitas. The first are the kind you marinate overnight and serve with an extensive array of side items. There are many good fajita marinade recipes that are simply too cumbersome when you're only cooking for one, or when you're in a time crunch. Try this quick version, substituting the chicken with extra lean ground beef or strips of flank steak if you wish.

Directions

Preheat nonstick skillet over medium heat Sauté chicken in lemon juice, liquid aminos or soy sauce (you can use leftover chicken breast) until heated through. Increase heat to medium-high to high heat and add onions and peppers, allowing them to char only slightly. Serve over bed of lettuce and top with salsa and fat-free sour cream if desired.

IN STELLA'S KITCHEN

Too busy to cook chicken? The next time you cook chicken, make extra to cut into strips and seal in freezer bags. These can easily defrost and be re-heated while cooking in a new recipe—significantly cheaper than the sodium-loaded pre-packaged versions sold in grocery stores.

Chicken Salad

This chicken salad calls for canned chicken breast because the recipe is meant to be quick. If you're the type who keeps pre-cooked chicken in the fridge, that's even better! Just tear or dice it fresh instead of using the canned chicken.

Directions

Mix all ingredients except lettuce together in small bowl. Serve mixture over the lettuce greens, or inside a whole-wheat pita.

Modifications

Make this into a perfect brunch item by omitting the onion, using fat-free plain or vanilla yogurt and adding one-half cup of green grapes. Serve in two cantaloupe halves.

2.5 servings

Ingredients

110-ounce can chicken breast meat

2 tablespoons fat-free mayonnaise
  (or fat-free plain yogurt)

1½ teaspoon Dijon
  or regular style mustard
  (omit if using yogurt)

¼ cup diced onion

¼ cup chopped celery

6 cups dark leafy greens,
  washed and torn

Nutritional Info
per serving

Calories—148.8

Carbohydrates—5.12g

Protein—28.4g

Fat—1.68g

Fiber—1.44g

4 servings

Ingredients

1 pound extra-lean
   ground turkey meat

2 egg whites, beaten

½ cup rolled oats

½ cup onion, finely chopped

¼ teaspoon garlic powder

½ cup celery, chopped

1 tablespoon spicy or
   Dijon style mustard

¼ teaspoon fresh ground pepper

1 teaspoon dried parsley

Sauce:

1 8-ounce can reduced-sodium
   tomato sauce (plain or Italian style)

Nutritional Info
per serving

Calories—178

Carbohydrates—9.3g

Protein—30.1g

Fat—2.1g

Fiber—1.8g

Leah's
Light and Lean Turkey Loaf

Instead of making your typical meatloaf, try swapping lean beef with extra-lean ground turkey. Serve this with some steamed broccoli and Garlic Smashed Potatoes (see page 141) or the Herbed New Potatoes from page 146.

Directions

Preheat oven 350 degrees. Mix all ingredients together in medium-sized bowl. Spoon mixture into an 8x8 square baking pan or loaf pan. Top loaf with tomato sauce. Bake for approximately 50 minutes. Makes four large slices.

IN STELLA'S KITCHEN

Cooking for one?—Many single people don't consider baking a loaf, casserole or soup dish to be a reasonable effort because they know there will be leftovers. Store leftovers in plastic compartment trays—add the meat, some leftover potatoes and broccoli to the containers. Freeze immediately for healthy, well-balanced frozen meals you can eat any time.

Lemon, Garlic and Herb Breast of Chicken

8 servings

This is a nice substitute for the battered and fried lemon chicken served in Chinese restaurants. It looks fancy when it's all laid out, making it suitable for entertaining—you don't have to tell how easy it was to prepare! This chicken will go well with broccoli and any type of rice, potato or pasta.

Ingredients

2 pounds boneless, skinless chicken breast cutlets

1 tablespoon minced garlic

¼ cup lemon juice

1½ tablespoon olive oil

2 tablespoons fresh chopped oregano (or 1 teaspoon dried)

2 tablespoons fresh chopped rosemary (or 1 teaspoon dried)

½ teaspoon fresh ground pepper

½ teaspoon salt replacement (such as Mrs. Dash)

3 lemons, cut into thick, round slices (set aside for later grilling)

Directions

Whisk lemon juice, olive oil and spices together in small bowl and set aside. Grill both sides of chicken cutlets by placing them length-wise across the grill. Transfer chicken to a serving platter. Place lemon slices on grill for a few minutes on each side to allow them to slightly char. Arrange lemon slices across chicken cutlets and pour sauce mixture over dish.

Note: This dish tastes best when the chicken has been cooked on a charcoal or gas grill. If you can't grill (and who says you can't fire up a gas grill in winter?), just broil the chicken.

Nutritional Info
per serving

Calories—151

Carbohydrates—2g

Protein—26.4g

Fat—4g

Fiber—.6g

6 servings

Ingredients

1½ pounds boneless, skinless, chicken breast, cut in small pieces

1 small green bell pepper, cubed

1 small red bell pepper, cubed

1 small yellow bell pepper, cubed

½ yellow onion, sliced

1 teaspoon crushed garlic

¼ cup reduced-sodium chicken broth

1 teaspoon liquid aminos or reduced-sodium soy sauce (optional)

Fresh ground pepper to taste

Nutritional Info
per serving

Calories—150

Carbohydrates—6.1g

Protein—27.6g

Fat—1.7g

Fiber—1.4g

Three-Pepper Chicken

It's surprising how much people will spend on packaged stir-fry mixes that are nothing more than frozen vegetables and heavily-salted sauce packets. The natural juices of the red, yellow and green peppers in this dish each have slightly different flavors and eliminate the need for excessive cooking oil or a heavy sauce. You may also notice that using a variety of peppers will add visual interest and the flavor complexity of a packaged sauce without the added sugar, salt or preservatives.

Directions

Preheat wok or large frying pan. Bring chicken broth and garlic to a simmer over medium heat. Add chicken and cook for about five minutes. Add the peppers and onion and cook until chicken is cooked through and vegetables are soft. Remove from heat and stir in liquid aminos or soy sauce and pepper. Serve over rice.

Low-Fat Chicken Piccata

Many versions of this recipe excessively bread the chicken or contain more butter than necessary for flavor. In a traditional piccatta, the breaded chicken is fried in oil or butter and then up to a half-cup of butter is used to make the sauce! To avoid that, this low-fat version of a classic Italian dish will require a revised method of preparation.

This is the only recipe in this book where you will be cooking the meat in a little bit of butter. By doing this, you'll maintain the traditional slight crispness to the chicken without having to bread more than necessary. Secondly, you'll have just enough butter flavor "stuck" to the chicken you won't notice it missing from the glaze—which we'll make separately to avoid washing out this effect. If you do like a heavier butter flavoring in the sauce itself, try using a little imitation butter flavoring (found near the vanilla extract at the supermarket) to avoid adding fat to the recipe.

Directions

Tenderize the chicken by placing it between two sheets of wax paper and pounding it with a meat tenderizer or rolling pin. Dip chicken in whole wheat or oat flour so that it is lightly dusted (you can dip in egg white or milk first if you'd like, but this is not necessary). Sauté chicken in butter until it has cooked through. Remove from pan and cover to keep it warm. Deglaze the pan with the white wine by pouring it in and allowing it to reduce (evaporate) for about one minute. Add lemon juice, broth, mushrooms and capers, and bring to a simmer. Remove from heat and stir in fresh chopped parsley. Pour this thin sauce over the chicken pieces and top with a few thin-cut lemon wedge slices.

4 servings

Ingredients

1 pound boneless, skinless chicken breasts

2 tablespoons whole wheat or oat flour

1 tablespoon butter or light olive oil

½ cup white wine

¼ cup lemon juice (fresh)

¼ cup reduced-sodium chicken broth

½ cup mushrooms, sliced thinly

2 tablespoons capers, drained

¼ cup fresh parsley, chopped

1 lemon, sliced in very thin wedges (for garnish)

Nutritional Info
per serving

Calories—173

Carbohydrates—5.1g

Protein—27.9g

Fat—4.5g

Fiber—.8g

Chicken and Broccoli

This is a healthy and super-easy method of preparing chicken and broccoli. The sauce for this is very light and is just enough for flavor. Use fresh broccoli so that you can appreciate the natural taste and texture of the food without the heavy gravies that are sometimes used by Chinese restaurants when they prepare this dish.

Directions

Sauté garlic in broth for one minute. Add chicken and cook until meat is no longer pink. Add the onion and broccoli and continue cooking until the broccoli has softened and onions are translucent.

Modifications

Try adding water chestnuts or bamboo shoots to this dish (drain before adding).

IN STELLA'S KITCHEN

Leftover broccoli? Cooked broccoli stores well in the fridge for up to five days if stored in a tightly covered dish.

---

6 servings

Ingredients

1½ pound boneless, skinless chicken breast, cut into strips or chunks

¾ cup onion, sliced

2 cups broccoli, chopped

1½ teaspoon minced garlic (about 3 cloves)

½ cup reduced-sodium chicken broth

Nutritional Info
per serving

Calories—130

Carbohydrates—2.1g

Protein—27g

Fat—1.5g

Fiber—.4g

Turkey Triano

Now you have something other than turkey sandwiches to make with Thanksgiving leftovers! This is a lean, lightly-breaded turkey just right for chicken parmesan or chicken-fried steak aficionados. The turkey cutlets are served with a wonderful white wine and cream sauce, fresh mushrooms and diced roma tomatoes.

Directions

Preheat oven to 375 degrees. Combine flour, ground pepper and half of the parsley in a medium bowl and mix well. Dip turkey cutlets in egg whites and then dip each side in the dry mixture until well coated. Spray both sides with nonstick cooking spray and bake cutlets for about 20–30 minutes or until coating is crisp and juices run clear. (Cooking time will vary; slices won't take as long.) While the turkey is cooking, heat a sauce pan or large skillet over medium-high heat. Bring white wine and onions to a simmer; add soup and remaining parsley. Reduce heat and cover. Allow sauce to simmer while turkey cooks. Serve turkey on a serving platter with sauce poured over the top. Garnish with tomato and mushroom slices.

IN STELLA'S KITCHEN

Leftover turkey? Leftover cooked turkey can be stored in the refrigerator for 3–4 days. If wrapped well, it can be stored in the freezer for 3–4 months.

4 servings

Ingredients

1 pound boneless turkey breast cutlets or slices

4 tablespoons whole-wheat flour

2 egg whites, beaten

¼ teaspoon fresh ground pepper

2 tablespoons fresh parsley (or 1 teaspoon dried)

1 can reduced-sodium, low-fat cream of mushroom soup

½ cup white table wine

2 tablespoons onions, diced finely

½ cup roma tomatoes, seeded and chopped

½ cup fresh mushrooms, sliced

Nutritional Info
per serving

Calories—224
Carbohydrates—17.2g
Protein—31.4g
Fat—3.3g
Fiber—2.8g

Ingredients

1½ pound boneless, skinless chicken breast, cut in chunks

1 medium red bell pepper, cut into strips

3 tablespoons natural peanut butter, chunky style

1 teaspoon Thai-style red curry paste

1 tablespoon chopped green onion

Nutritional Info
per serving

Calories—175

Carbohydrates—3.3g

Protein—28.3g

Fat—5.5g

Fiber—1g

Spicy Thai Peanut Chicken

If you're a Pad Thai fan, you'll appreciate this super-fast dish that has a similar flavor. You can make it as hot as you'd like by simply adding more Thai Red Curry paste—this stuff is hot. You may wish to add some of your other favorite vegetables to this if time permits. Serve on top of salad or with steamed rice.

Directions

Spray wok or nonstick frying pan with cooking spray or several squirts of lime juice. Sauté the chicken and red pepper until chicken is cooked through. Add peanut butter, Thai curry paste and a small amount of water to reach desired consistency. Cook until hot, stir in green onions and serve.

IN STELLA'S KITCHEN

Too spicy? When you've overspiced a dish and find it's too hot to eat, try counteracting the heat with sweet. Use a little bit of artificial sweetner to help overcome the heat, or consider adding more vegetables to the dish.

Tomasita's Chicken Tortilla Stew

This wonderful high-protein, high-fiber soup is so light it can be eaten any time of year. Don't limit yourself to the vegetables in the recipes—be creative and use your favorites!

Directions

Preheat oven 350 degrees. Spray both sides of the corn tortillas with nonstick cooking spray and cut into thin strips. Bake until crispy, turning a few times to toast them evenly. Remove from oven and set aside. In large soup pot, bring broth to a boil. Add onions, garlic, peppers and potatoes and cook for about five minutes or until peppers begin to soften. Add chicken, corn, stewed tomatoes and spices. Bring to a boil for another five minutes and reduce to a simmer until ready to serve. Garnish with a few tortilla strips and freshly squeezed lime wedges.

12 servings

Ingredients

2 pounds boneless, skinless chicken breasts, cubed

4 cups (32 ounces) fat-free, reduced-sodium chicken broth

1 cup green bell pepper, diced (about 1 large pepper)

¾ cup red bell pepper, diced

6 cloves garlic, minced

2 14-ounce cans Mexican-style stewed tomatoes

1 jalapeno pepper, diced (or more)

3 green Anaheim chile peppers, diced

1 cup yellow onion, sliced (about 1)

1 cup potato, cubed (optional)

1 14-ounce can unsalted corn, drained

1 teaspoon ground cumin

½ teaspoon fresh ground pepper

1 tablespoon fresh cilantro

Tortilla garnish:

4 corn tortillas, 4 limes (wedged)

Nutritional Info
per serving

Calories—203

Carbohydrates—21.9g

Protein—23.9g

Fat—2.3g

Fiber—3g

Green Chile Chicken Stew

6 servings

Ingredients

1½ pounds boneless, skinless chicken breasts, cubed

1 cup reduced-sodium fat free chicken broth

1 can yellow corn (sodium-free), drained

Wito's Skillet-Roasted Green Chile (see page 160)

Nutritional Info
per serving

Calories—203

Carbohydrates—13.3

Protein—31g

Fat—2.8g

Fiber—1g

This very simple stew will satisfy the urgings of green chile fans who want to substitute the pork of traditional green chile. It's delicious alone or served over rice. You'll be surprised how satisfying this is without the requisite fattening side items that often accompany Mexican food.

Directions

Prepare Skillet Roasted Green Chile as instructed, which can be made ahead of time and refrigerated or frozen. Bring broth to a boil and add chicken. Cook until chicken is cooked through. Add the green chile and corn and reduce heat. Simmer on low until ready to serve. Sprinkle with reduced-fat cheddar or Monterey jack or a dollop of fat-free sour cream if desired.

Modifications

You can substitute chicken with 96% lean ground beef for an equally pleasing dish.

Everyday Chicken Picks

While this cookbook provides a wealth of easy-to-prepare chicken dishes, there are times when even chopping up vegetables is too time consuming. These suggestions are suitable for everyday chicken and do not call for any special ingredients.

Tobasco:	Tabasco sauce, garlic powder, onion powder and black pepper
Italian:	Add a variety of Italian herbs (rosemary, basil, tarragon, arugula) and/or a few tablespoons of stewed tomatoes
Lemon-Pepper:	Use salt-free lemon-pepper seasoning or squeeze real lemon and pepper onto the chicken
Lemon-Dill:	Use salt-free lemon-pepper seasoning and dill or squeeze real lemon juice, dill and pepper onto the chicken
Vinaigrette:	Use a tablespoon Balsamic vinegar or Balsamic dressing per 4-ounce portion of chicken
Spicy Tex-Mex:	Use prepared salsa or chili powder
Garlic-Pepper:	Crushed garlic, garlic powder or minced garlic (from a jar) and fresh ground pepper
Lemon-Rosemary:	Lemon juice, rosemary and a bit of garlic powder

3

Fish Fare

An estimated 80% of the American public eats a diet deficient in essential fatty acids (EFAs), the fats necessary for optimal function of cells, nerves, organs and muscle tissue. From this standpoint, the Omega-3 oils present in fish are one of the best sources of EFAs that can be incorporated into our diets.

With the exception of canned tuna, it's hard to convince people that cooking fish is regular, weekday fare, rather than reserved solely for special meals. This is often because many people do not realize how easy it is to cook.

There is a saying that if you teach a man to fish, you help feed him for a lifetime. While the fish recipes in this chapter will do you no good out on the water, they *will* help you receive a lifetime its dietary benefits by teaching you how easily it can be prepared.

3

Fish Fare

Grilled Teriyaki Salmon

Tuna Melt Patties

It's Tuna Time!

Fresh Shrimp and Broccoli

Grilled Shrimp Kabobs

General Tsang's Spicy Dipping Shrimp

Summer Shrimp and Pasta Toss

Baja Mahi-Mahi

Salmon with Roasted Pepper Salsa

Thai Peanut Shrimp

Shrimp and Avocado Salad

Chilled Lobster Salad

Salmon Stuffed Tomatoes

Grilled Teriyaki Salmon

4 servings

Sometimes it's the simplest dish that can win a life over to healthier eating. Indulge yourself with a special treat by allowing this teriyaki salmon dish to marinate overnight and toasting the sesame seeds in a pan prior to adding to the teriyaki.

Directions

Combine soy, garlic, juice, bourbon and ginger in a small bowl and whisk together. Marinate salmon in mixture for at least 20 minutes, overnight if possible. While the fish is marinating, prepare the rice or a salad sidedish if desired. Reserve leftover marinade for glazing in small saucepan. Stir in sesame seeds and green onions and cook over very low heat until just before ready to serve the salmon. Just before serving, bring marinade to a boil for a few minutes to allow it to reduce and thicken. Grill or bake salmon for five to seven minutes per side, grilling with the skin side up first (if filet has skin). Be sure to lay a small piece of foil down on the grilling surface if you're grilling outdoors. Serve salmon with a spoonful of hot teriyaki glaze drizzled over the top.

Modifications

No juice? The brown sugar or honey traditionally added to teriyaki for sweetness has been replaced by the natural fructose in apple juice. The light acidic nature of the apple juice doubles as a tenderizing agent as well. However, you can replace the apple juice with equal amounts of bourbon and reduced-sodium soy and two packets of artificial sweetener if you prefer.

Ingredients

1 pound salmon filets

¼ cup reduced-sodium soy sauce

1½ teaspoon crushed garlic (about 3 cloves)

3 tablespoons apple juice

3 tablespoons Kentucky bourbon (may substitute with lemon juice)

¼ teaspoon ground ginger

3 tablespoons green onions, chopped

1 teaspoon sesame seeds (optional)

Nutritional Info
per serving

Calories—214.75

Carbohydrates—4g

Protein—25.5g

Fat—7.25g

Fiber—trace

Tuna Melt Patties

Ingredients

1 6-ounce can tuna, drained

1 egg white, beaten

2 tablespoons oatmeal
(quick or regular)

2 tablespoons onion, diced
(or ¼ teaspoon onion powder)

¼ teaspoon garlic powder

Salt or salt substitute and
pepper to taste

2 tablespoons reduced-fat
mozzarella (optional)

Nutritional Info
per serving

Calories—146.5

Carbohydrates—4.5g

Protein—25.5g

Fat—2g

Fiber—.5g

This special edition of an American classic clocks in at a preparation speed of under five minutes.

Directions

Mix all ingredients except cheese together in a small bowl. Heat a small nonstick frying pan over medium heat and spray with nonstick cooking spray. Make two small patties by spooning half the tuna mixture into each side of the pan and lightly pressing with fork to flatten into a patty. Cook until both sides are brown. Top with one tablespoon cheese and serve alone, on top of light bread, or with your sides of choice.

Modifications

See "Tuna Time" on the next page for more ideas on how you can season your tuna patties.

It's Tuna Time!

Tuna has long been a favorite protein source for muscle builders, dieters and athletes. It's cheap, fast, portable and pre-portioned in convenient sizes. Did I mention it was cheap? The fact is, it *is* a great source of protein and omega-3 essential fats *and* it makes a great snack too. Solid white albacore can taste great all by itself if it fits your budget. If not, here are a few "straight outta the can" recipes you can use to bring a little life into your next can of chunk tuna, or even canned chicken. For variety, salmon may be used in these simple combinations.

Lemon-Pepper Tuna: Lemon juice and fresh ground pepper or sprinkle with lemon pepper seasoning

Balsamic Tuna: Balsamic vinegar and fresh ground pepper

Mustard-Dill Tuna: Dill, 1 tablespoon mustard and chopped celery

Southwest Tuna: 1 tablespoon nonfat mayo, ¼ of an Anaheim green chile, black pepper

Honey-Mustard Tuna: 1–2 tablespoons honey mustard

Tuna Fried Rice: Sauté cooked brown rice, chopped green or yellow onions and egg whites in pan sprayed with butter flavored nonstick spray. Mix in tuna and serve.

Tuna-Stuffed Tomato: Mix 1 tablespoon nonfat mayo, pepper and tuna and stuff inside a tomato. Top tomato with a slice of mozzarella cheese and bake in a toaster oven until the cheese melts.

Old El Paso Tuna: 1 heaping tablespoon salsa or 1 tablespoon chopped green chile peppers

Tuna Italiano: 1 tablespoon Italian dressing or olive oil vinaigrette, fresh ground pepper

Tuna Piccata: 1 teaspoon capers, lemon juice, ½ teaspoon parsley, fresh ground pepper

All-American Tuna: 1 tablespoon fat-free mayo, 1 chopped pickle, ½ stalk chopped celery or onion

Texas Tuna: 1 tablespoon BBQ sauce

Tuna Melt: 1 tablespoon fat-free mayo, 1 ounce cheese melted on top

Tuna Parmesan: Mix in 1 tablespoon catsup, tomato sauce or spaghetti sauce. Sprinkle with breadcrumbs or a crushed cracker, top with 1 ounce low-fat mozzarella cheese. Cook in microwave or toaster oven until cheese melts.

No-Time Tuna: 1 fork, 1 glass of water

Ingredients

1 pound medium shrimp,
  peeled and de-veined

½ cup onion, sliced

2 cups broccoli, chopped

1½ teaspoon minced garlic
 (about 3 cloves)

¾ cup snow peas,
  fresh or frozen and thawed

½ cup reduced-sodium
  chicken broth

Nutritional Info
per serving

Calories—153

Carbohydrates—7g

Protein—26g

Fat—2.3g

Fiber—23g

Fresh
Shrimp and Broccoli

No need to order out when you can prepare your own
stir-fry dishes at home!

Directions

Sauté garlic in broth for one minute. Add shrimp and
vegetables and continue simmering until shrimp is white,
broccoli has softened and onions are translucent.

Modifications

Try adding drained, canned water chestnuts, bamboo
shoots, or bean sprouts to this dish.

Grilled Shrimp Kabobs

Try serving this succulently marinated "Shrimp on the Barbie" at your next barbeque.

Directions

Whisk all marinade ingredients together in a glass bowl and set aside. Marinate shrimp for at least 20 minutes, or overnight if possible. To cook, heat preheat grill and place alternating pieces of shrimp, vegetables and pineapple chunks on the skewer sticks. Grill until shrimp are cooked through and serve.

IN STELLA'S KITCHEN

Safe marinating—Making leftover marinade into a light sauce to drizzle over dishes is a great idea. However, you should always boil the marinade for about five minutes to destroy any possible bacteria.

4 servings

Ingredients

1 pound large shrimp, peeled and de-veined

1 large onion, cut in chunks

1 small red bell pepper, cubed

1 small green bell pepper, cubed

½ cup pineapple chunks (fresh or packed in its own juice)

4–8 skewers (soak wooden skewers overnight)

Marinade:
¼ cup reduced-sodium soy sauce

½ teaspoon ground ginger

3 cloves of garlic finely chopped

3 ounces light beer

1 tablespoon onion powder

Nutritional Info
per serving

Calories—173

Carbohydrates—13.4g

Protein—24.7g

Fat—2.3g

Fiber—2.4g

General Tsang's Spicy Dipping Shrimp

8 servings

Ingredients

2 pounds medium or large shrimp, cooked, peeled and de-veined

1 cup reduced-sodium tomato sauce

3 tablespoons lemon juice

2/3 cup tomato, diced and seeded

1 medium jalapeno, diced

1 teaspoon cayenne pepper

2 teaspoons Tabasco or other hot sauce

1 teaspoon garlic powder

½ teaspoon salt

½ teaspoon black pepper

1 tablespoon fresh cilantro, chopped

Nutritional Info
per serving

Calories—136

Carbohydrates—5g

Protein—23.75g

Fat—2.12g

Fiber—.62g

Here's a spicy shrimp cocktail that packs a lot of heat in a small package.

Directions

Combine all ingredients except tomatoes and shrimp together in a small bowl and whisk until well blended. Stir in tomatoes. Refrigerate in a glass dish until ready to serve. Arrange shrimp in glass bowl or cocktail glasses filled with crushed iced and serve with small sides of cocktail sauce, lemon wedges and finger napkins.

IN STELLA'S KITCHEN

Special occasions—Once in a while it's fun to splurge on special ingredients. Try using large prawns instead of shrimp in dishes that call for smaller-sized shrimp.

Summer Shrimp and Pasta Toss

This light, summertime shrimp and vegetable salad tastes great hot or cold while it provides a full spectrum of protein, carbohydrates, fat and nutrients.

Directions

Cook pasta al dente according to package directions, drain and set aside. Preheat a large wok or pan over medium heat. Sauté garlic in light olive oil until light brown and add shrimp and onion. Cook until onion begins to soften. Add zucchini, squash and red pepper and cook until zucchini and squash are slightly soft. Add pasta to pan, toss everything together until pasta is hot and serve.

IN STELLA'S KITCHEN

Food facts—According to the USDA Nutrient Guidelines, red peppers place in the top five vegetables for the highest amounts of the antioxidant vitamin C. Use them regularly in your favorite salsa or stir-fry recipe.

6 servings

Ingredients

8 ounces ziti or penne pasta

1 pound medium shrimp, peeled and de-veined

½ tablespoon light olive oil

2 tablespoons minced garlic

¼ cup lemon juice

¾ cup red bell pepper, diced

¾ cup yellow squash, cut into strips

¾ cup zucchini, sliced

½ cup red onion, sliced

1½ tablespoon fresh basil, chopped (or 1½ teaspoon dried herb)

Nutritional info
per serving

Calories—246.8

Carbohydrates—33.5g

Protein—21g

Fat—3.3g

Fiber—2.97g

Baja Mahi-Mahi

Surf's up! Experience a spicy taste of the Baja with this grilled mahi-mahi topped with a zingy and easy-to-make fresh salsa.

Ingredients

1 pound mahi-mahi steaks,
cut ½-¾" thick

1¼ cup diced tomato
(about 1 large tomato)

1 teaspoon olive oil

1 clove minced garlic

1 tablespoon fresh cilantro

¼ cup yellow bell pepper, diced

2½ tablespoons lime juice

1 teaspoon diced jalapeno
(fresh or canned)

1 dash Tabasco or hot pepper sauce

Directions

Prepare salsa by combining vegetables, lime juice, cilantro, garlic and olive oil in small bowl. Allow the salsa to rest in the refrigerator overnight or as long as possible. Sprinkle fish with pepper and salt and grill for five or six minutes per side on outdoor or indoor grill. Top with chilled salsa.

Modifications

Use green chile in place of the jalapeno for a milder marinade. If you buy your chile peppers fresh, look for Anaheim chile peppers.

IN STELLA'S KITCHEN

Chef's note—Mahi-mahi sometimes has a darker lateral band of flesh coursing through it. The flavor of this darker meat is sometimes very intense so you may wish to remove it.

Nutritional Info
per serving

Calories—123

Carbohydrates—4.25g

Protein—20.5g

Fat—2.5g

Fiber—.75g

Salmon
with Roasted Pepper Salsa

4 servings

Something tells me you may miss out on this tender, grilled salmon with roasted red pepper salsa because it requires grilled vegetables. Rather than skip this terrific meal, try making this on an indoor grilling machine. You'll be amazed at what you can do in 20 minutes.

Directions

Preheat indoor grilling machine. Spray large chunks of onions and bell peppers with nonstick cooking spray and spread across grill. Close the top lid of grill and allow vegetables to grill until onions are soft and peppers are blistered. Remove vegetables from heat and wrap in foil or seal in a plastic bag. Lightly spray the bottom portion of grill with nonstick cooking spray.

Next, sprinkle the salmon with pepper. Grill, skin side up for approximately five to seven minutes depending on thickness. Do not close the lid.* Flip salmon over and cook, skin side down, for another five to seven minutes. While the second side is grilling, remove roasted vegetables from bag, peel skin off peppers and discard. Chop peppers and onions and combine in small bowl with Balsamic vinegar and basil.

Remove salmon from grill. The skin will most likely stick to the grill; remove it before serving if this does not occur. Serve salmon on bed of rice, mixed greens or with a sweet potato. Top with salsa. And next time, be bold and try this recipe on your outdoor grill using a vegetable grilling pan.

*Chef's Note: You certainly *can* close the lid of the grill to accelerate cooking time of the fish. In this instance, though, the pressure of the lid will force out the natural juices of the fish. While removing extra fat in this manner is an integral function of the indoor grill's design, the Omega-3 EFAs in the salmon are valuable dietary fats. It just makes sense to lock the juices in and enjoy the resulting tenderness while you wait for the pepper skins to steam off in the plastic bag.

Ingredients

1 pound salmon fillets

1 red bell pepper, cut in large pieces

1 green bell pepper, cut in large pieces

1 medium red onion, cut in large pieces

2½ tablespoons Balsamic vinegar

5 leaves fresh basil, chopped

Nutritional Info
per serving

Calories—196
Carbohydrates—7.75g
Protein—25.25g
Fat—6.75g
Fiber—1.95g

Thai Peanut Shrimp

4 servings

Ingredients

1 pound large shrimp,
  peeled and de-veined

½ cup red bell pepper, diced

½ cup green bell pepper, diced

3 tablespoons natural peanut butter,
  chunky style

1 teaspoon Thai-style red curry paste

1 tablespoon chopped green onion

One of the nice things about shrimp is how fast it both thaws and cooks. You can use fresh or frozen shrimp in this recipe and serve with brown rice, on a bed of mixed greens as part of a delicious salad, or even alone as an spicy appetizer.

Directions

Spray wok or nonstick frying pan with cooking spray or several squirts of lime juice. Sauté shrimp and red and green pepper until shrimp loses its translusence. Add the peanut butter, Thai curry paste and a small amount of water to reach desired consistency. Cook until hot, stir in green onions and serve.

Modifications

If you're having company, why not double this recipe and use half chicken and half shrimp for a more interesting main dish?

Nutritional Info
per serving

Calories—201

Carbohydrates—5.9g

Protein—26.1g

Fat—8g

Fiber—1.3g

Shrimp and Avocado Salad

Fans of "California Roll" sushi will enjoy this nutritious and colorful shrimp salad.

Directions

Toss all ingredients except greens and avocado together in a large bowl. Place a scoop of the mixture on a bed of greens and garnish with lemon wedges and avocado chunks or a dollop of the Guacamole Lijera (Lean Guacamole) from page 165.

IN STELLA'S KITCHEN

Cracking up? If you find shelling or cracking cooked shellfish difficult, try boiling it in water and one tablespoone of white wine.

Ingredients

1 pound small or medium salad shrimp (cooked and peeled)

$^1/_3$ cup frozen yellow corn, thawed

½ cup green pepper, diced

½ cup red pepper, diced

½ cup cherry tomatoes (or diced and seeded chopped tomato)

3 tablespoons lemon juice (or serve with lemon wedges)

1 tablespoon olive oil

2 tablespoons green onion, chopped fine

½ cup avocado, diced (or try the Guacamole Lijera on page 165)

8 cups romaine, bibb or red leaf lettuce (about 12 leaves or one medium head)

Salt substitute and pepper to taste

Nutritional Info
per serving

Calories—225.5

Carbohydrates—12.25g

Protein—26.25g

Fat—8.75g

Fiber—3.22g

Chilled Lobster Salad

4 servings

Ingredients

8 ounces penne pasta,
  dry (4 servings)

2 teaspoons light olive oil

2 tablespoons fresh basil, chopped
  (or 2 teaspoons dried herb)

2 cloves garlic, crushed

1 pound lobster, cooked and
  chopped

$1/3$ cup nonfat plain yogurt

1 tablespoon fresh dill weed
  (or 1teaspoon dried herb)

Pepper to taste

Nutritional Info
per serving

Calories—342

Carbohydrates—44.5g

Protein—31g

Fat—4g

Fiber—2.7g

If you're looking for a special treat that can be enjoyed out on the deck as the sun goes down, you'll love this chilled pasta salad. Consider pre-cooked lobster or crab meat if you want to save time.

Directions

Cook pasta to al dente, rinse with cool water and set aside. Sauté garlic in light olive oil until brown. Toss pasta into oil and garlic mixture, then add basil. Cover and refrigerate while preparing lobster. To prepare the lobster, combine all remaining ingredients in a medium bowl until well blended and refrigerate until cool or ready to serve. Transfer pasta to large serving platter and top with lobster salad mixture to serve.

Modifications

Crab: Substitute equal amount of cooked crab meat in place of lobster.

Low-carb: Omit pasta and prepare lobster as directed. Serve lobster on a bed of tossed greens.

IN STELLA'S KITCHEN

Making magic at mealtime—Train your brain to associate meal times with people, not just food. Even if your family dinner only took 20 minutes to prepare, turn off the TV, dim the lights and maybe even light a few candles. The calm setting can be a romantic or fun way to unwind and connect with your loved ones. Your whole family will enjoy your great preparations more, too!

Salmon Stuffed Tomatoes

Looking to add EFAs to your diet? Try these tomatoes filled with salmon instead of the usual canned tuna—preparation time: 20 minutes.

Directions

Cook brown rice according to package directions and set aside. Grill salmon on indoor grill while preparing vegetables. To prepare tomatoes for stuffing, slice off the top third and scoop out the seeds with a spoon. Whisk olive oil, mustard and lemon together in a large bowl. Stir in rice and corn. Once salmon is cooked, remove it from heat and flake it with a fork. Add salmon to the rice and corn mixture and blend well. Stuff each tomato with equal amounts salmon mixture and serve.

Modifications

If you like canned salmon, you might substitute drained, canned salmon in this recipe.

4 servings

Ingredients

1 pound fresh salmon, cooked

$1/_3$ cup instant brown rice (dry)

2 tablespoons lemon juice, white wine or white wine vinegar

1½ teaspoon Dijon or spicy brown mustard

1 teaspoon olive oil

1 teaspoon dried parsley

½ cup frozen corn kernels (or drained, no-sodium-added canned corn)

4 large tomatoes, tops removed and seeded

Nutritional Info
per serving

Calories—271g
Carbohydrates—21.5g
Protein—27.5g
Fat—9g
Fiber—3.12g

4

Breakfast Basics

While you slept soundly, your miraculous body spent the night repairing cells and muscle tissue, growing stronger. A critical component of successful athletic performance and a healthy body is feeding the body a continuous stream of nutrients throughout the day. Breakfast is an especially important part of this process because it is the meal installment charged with replenishing a body that has fed off its energy and protein stores for a span of seven or more hours. In spite of this, it's not difficult to notice that for far too many wonderful people a nutritious breakfast is an unimportant concern.

When you shop, look at the labels of the cereals aimed at our children and peer into the busy coffee shop next door to see what's become of the concept of breakfast. What do you see? People who "didn't have time" to eat breakfast are standing in long lines to purchase huge bagels and overpriced coffee with more calories than a hamburger and more sugar than a candy bar. This is a tragic illustration of what the breakfast meal is becoming—an injection of nutrient-poor white flour products fortified with refined sugar.

For those who seriously want to lead a healthy lifestyle and pursue energetic activities, this poor nutritional attitude is not acceptable. The sample breakfast above does not propel one towards general health, much less physical excellence. These recipes that follow are either protein rich or dense with complex carbohydrates, and naturally fortified with the nutrients that meet our needs for taste and fast preparation, and our bodies' rigorous standards for nourishment.

4

Breakfast Basics

Eat Your Oatmeal

One of the best quick breakfasts you can prepare is a bowl of oatmeal. Not only is it economically priced and easy to make, it's also versatile. Instead of buying a box of 10 packets for twice the price of a large container, try some of these delicious and frugal ideas. These oatmeal variations pack more energy and flavor than pre-packaged oats without the 13 or more grams of refined sugar.

Apple-Cinnamon: Add chopped apple or a few teaspoons of natural, unsweetened applesauce to oatmeal and cook. Sprinkle with cinnamon.

Maple and Brown Sugar: Instead of real brown sugar, you can use sugar-free pancake syrup and a dash of cinnamon. There is also a brown sugar replacement newly available.

Fruit and Cream: Add a little milk or vanilla protein powder and a few strawberries or blueberries to oatmeal, or mix in a teaspoon of sugar-free preserves.

Maple-Walnut: Add 1 tablespoon sugar-free pancake syrup and a few chopped walnuts.

French Vanilla: Add 1 teaspoon vanilla, a splash of low-fat milk and a packet of Splenda.

Cinnamon-Raisin: Try using a few dashes of cinnamon, a splash of sugar-free maple syrup and a teaspoon of raisins instead of flavored packets.

Protein Boost: Stir in 1 scoop of your favorite protein powder.

Butter-Pecan: Add a drip of imitation butter flavor, teaspoon of butter substitute or a few sprinkles of Butter Buds and a teaspoon of chopped pecans.

Other Grains: Try a multi-grain hot cereal, 5- or 7-grain hot cereal, or oat bran for a little change of pace. Any of the flavor varieties listed above work well with these complex carbohydrate hot cereals.

Oatmeal on the go?

If you buy oatmeal in packets under the guise of convenience, remember they only contain a third of a cup of oatmeal. A snack-sized sandwich bag has just enough room for a true half-cup-sized serving of oatmeal. You can quickly pack a few with no need to measure, and store them in the pantry for days when you need to grab and go.

Ingredients

- ⅓ cup cup low-fat soy flour
- ⅓ cup corn meal
- 1 cup brown rice flour
- ¼ cup Howard's Sugar-Free Maple syrup
- 4 egg whites
- ½ cup natural applesauce
- 1 cup fat-free plain yogurt
- 1½ teaspoon vanilla
- ¾ teaspoon salt
- 4 packets Splenda (optional, use only if you like sweet muffins)
- 1 teaspoon baking powder
- ½ cup dried cranberries
- ⅓ cup chopped almonds
- ⅓ cup sliced almonds (for tops of muffins)

Nutritional Info
per serving

Calories—166

Carbohydrates—22g

Protein—11g

Fat—3.4g

Fiber—1.25g

Cranberry-Almond Breakfast Muffins

This is an old favorite muffin recipe with a modern makeover. It's been re-vamped to increase the protein and fiber content and omit the sugar of the original recipe. Instead of nutrient-poor white flour, this recipe uses natural, unprocessed alternatives. Served with a protein shake and you have a perfect breakfast to go.

Directions

Preheat oven to 350 degrees. Mix all dry ingredients, cranberries and chopped almonds in a medium-sized bowl. Mix the remaining ingredients in a seperate bowl before adding to dry mixture. The batter will be lumpy. Spoon batter into muffin tins lined with paper cups or sprayed with nonstick cooking spray, filling them half-way. Garnish the top of each muffin with slivered almonds and a few cranberries. Bake until golden brown and almonds appear toasted (about 20 mins).

Modifications

Cinnamon-Raisin Muffins: Replace cranberries with an equal measure of raisins, add 1 teaspoon cinnamon, replace cornmeal with equal amount of oatmeal.

Lower carb version: Omit the cranberries to subtract four grams of carbohydrates per muffin from nutritional counts.

IN STELLA'S KITCHEN

Eating on the run—Nutritious breakfast muffins are easy to freeze and great for eating on the run. Freeze muffins in a plastic zip-lock bag or airtight container. Muffins can be quickly defrosted in the microwave in a plastic baggie to maintain their softness.

Omelet Supremo

Omelets are more than a Sunday morning pleasure, they're also a perfect way to consume protein when you're in a hurry. This particular omelet illustrates the common sense of learning to prepare breakfasts that are simple to make in a few minutes.

Directions

Beat eggs and egg whites together and cook in skillet sprayed with nonstick cooking spray. Top with cheese and season with red pepper flakes.

IN STELLA'S KITCHEN

Did you know? The little stringy cords (chalazae) in egg whites are what anchor the yolk in the center of the egg? If the chalazae are bigger, it means the egg is fresher.

1 serving

Ingredients

2 whole eggs

4 egg whites

1 slice (1 ounce) low-fat Muenster cheese

Red pepper flakes to taste

Nutritional Info
per serving

Calories—292

Carbohydrates—4g

Protein—33g

Fat—15g

Fiber—0g

Southwest Chicken Fajita Omelet

Ingredients

3 ounces boneless, skinless chicken breast

5 egg whites plus 1 whole egg, beaten together with fork

½ green pepper, cut in strips

¼ cup onion, sliced

Dash of soy sauce

2 tablespoons salsa

Nutritional Info
per serving

Calories—308

Carbohydrates—15g

Protein— 43g

Fat— 7g

Fiber—2.3g

Here's a protein-packed taste of the Southwest that can be eaten any time of day. You really don't need to worry about marinating the chicken or otherwise over-complicating this recipe. It can also be made using restaurant or home-cooked fajita leftovers.

Directions

Spray nonstick pan with cooking spray and sauté chicken breast, dash of soy and onions until chicken is cooked through. Add green pepper and one tablespoon of the salsa and continue to cook until green peppers are slightly softened. Move to side of pan while eggs cook. Once the egg mixture has cooked through, move to plate and spoon remaining salsa on top. Garnish with low-fat cheese or fat-free sour cream if desired.

IN STELLA'S KITCHEN

Prepare ahead—Chicken breast strips can be cooked ahead of time and refrigerated or can be frozen in small portions for quick use in omelets, stirfrys and salads.

Four Corners Baked Frittata

If you've never eaten a frittata, it is similar to a quiche without the crust or an open-faced omelet. This southwestern inspired frittata is easily prepared and great for weekend breakfasts or feeding special guests who may be staying at your homes for the holidays.

Directions

Preheat oven to 375 degrees. Mix corn, green chiles, and onion together in a small bowl and spread on the bottom of a 9x12 inch baking dish or two 9-inch pie plates sprayed with non-stick cooking spray. Spread diced chicken over the green chile, onion, and onion mixture. Whisk eggs, egg whites, yogurt, and skim milk together and pour over pan. Top frittata with grated cheese and sprinkle with parsley and oregano. Bake for about 30 minutes or until firm and golden.

Modifications

All-American Frittata: Replace corn and green chile with 2 ½ cups fresh or thawed broccoli or spinach.

Vegetable Frittata: Omit corn, green chiles, and chicken and replace with 3 ½ cups diced vegetables of choice (bell peppers, mushrooms, tomatoes, onions).

8 servings

Ingredients

7 whole eggs

6 large egg whites

2 cups cooked boneless, skinless chicken breast, diced

1 cup canned corn, drained

¼ cup onion, diced

¾ cup diced green chile peppers, drained

¼ cup plain, nonfat yogurt

½ cup skim milk

1 cup part-skim, reduced-fat Mozzarella cheese

1 teaspoon dried parsley

1 teaspoon dried oregano

Salt or salt substitute to taste

Nutritional Info
per serving

Calories—208

Carbohydrates—9.3g

Protein—23.8g

Fat—8.5g

Fiber—.8g

Low-Carb Pancakes

Ingredients

10 egg whites

¼ cup unprocessed bran flakes

1 packet artificial sweetener

A dash of cinnamon

The unprocessed bran flakes in this recipe add a little dignity to these low-carb pancakes. The high fiber content of the bran drops the effective carb count to just six grams. These are a nice, fluffy alternative to plain egg whites and expensive low-carb pancake mixes.

Directions

Whip egg whites with a hand mixer until a stiff foam develops. (If you neglect to do this, your pancakes will have a flat, omelet-like texture.) Add the remaining ingredients and mix well. The batter will be foamy. Spray skillet with nonstick cooking spray and spoon in batter. Cook until each side is lightly browned. Serve with a butter replacement and sugar-free syrup if desired.

Nutritional Info
per serving

Calories—192

Carbohydrates—12g

Protein—37g

Fat—0g

Fiber—6g

Protein-Fortified Waffles

Store-bought frozen waffles or mixes, even those marketed as "whole wheat," are made mostly with nutrient-poor white flour. This waffle version packs a wallop of nutritious, low-glycemic, complex carbohydrates and has received a boost of protein.

Directions

Whisk all ingredients in small bowl. Spoon batter into preheated waffle iron sprayed with nonstick cooking spray. Cook until golden brown and serve with sugar-free syrup, sugar-free preserves or fresh cut strawberries.

*The brand of protein used in this recipe contains 200 calories, 4 g carb, 44 g protein, 2 g fat, and 2 g fiber.

IN STELLA'S KITCHEN

Saving money—Make your own oat flour: You can purchase oat flour at a reasonable cost but you can also make your own quite easily: Grind oats in your blender or food processor.

1 serving

Ingredients

3 egg whites

¼ cup oat flour

1 scoop vanilla protein powder*

1 tablespoon natural applesauce

1 packet artificial sweetener

A dash cinnamon (optional)

Nutritional Info
per serving

Calories—235
Carbohydrates—8g
Protein—35g
Fat—3g
Fiber—2g

Basic Egg White Pancakes

Ingredients

8 egg whites

½ cup oatmeal (or oat bran)

1 packet Splenda
or other artificial sweetener

A dash cinnamon

Nutritional Info
per serving

Calories—282

Carbohydrates—30g

Protein—33g

Fat—2.5g

Fiber—4g

There are many variations of the protein powerhouse egg white pancake. It's pretty likely the more complicated the recipe, the less likely you will be to consume the easily-assimilated protein found in egg whites. This simple recipe for egg white pancakes that can be prepared ahead of time and easily warmed up in the microwave or modified on days when you have extra time.

Directions

Whisk all ingredients. Cook in nonstick skillet until both sides are golden brown. If you'd like them to be a little fluffier, try beating the egg whites to a stiff foam before adding the oat bran. Serve with butter replacement spread and sugar-free pancake syrup if desired.

Modifications

For a little variety, try adding chopped fresh or frozen strawberries or blueberries, sugar-free preserves, a little tofu or cottage cheese to the batter.

IN STELLA'S KITCHEN

In a hurry? If you get a late start, you don't have to skip breakfast. Make a modified version of the recipe above. Spray a pan with nonstick cooking spray, stir in the egg whites and sprinkle the oatmeal over the eggs. Flip once to brown both sides, spread with a little natural peanut butter, Splenda, or sugar-free preserves, fold in half and eat on the way out the door.

Hearty Oatmeal Pancakes

Pancake mixes use just enough whole wheat flour to take advantage of an unsuspecting consumer who doesn't notice that "white flour" is one of the main ingredients. The recipe below is devoid of white flour and is actually cheaper to make because it can be made from ingredients you've already got in your cupboards. The oats in this recipe provide an extended source of energy and a special taste that comes only with the effort of cooking from scratch.

Directions

Heat milk (or water) until hot; stir in oats and set aside. Beat egg whites into a stiff foam with hand mixer or blender and reserve. Mix the remaining dry ingredients together and stir in oatmeal/milk mixture and oil (if used). Fold in egg whites until mixture is well blended. Spray pan with nonstick spray and cook pancakes until browned on both sides.

Chef's Note: Beating the egg whites into a stiff foam is what makes these pancakes so fluffy. If you do not have a hand mixer or blender, whisk the whites as best you can.

Modifications

Blueberry pancakes: Add ¼ cup blueberries (fresh or thawed) to recipe, omit cinnamon

Oat-nut pancakes: Add 1½ tablespoon diced pecans, walnuts or almonds to recipe.

Whole grain pancakes: Replace quick oats with multigrain hot cereal.

IN STELLA'S KITCHEN

Double do it—When preparing good food like these oatmeal pancakes, it's a smart idea to double the recipe and freeze the extra portions in individual measures. This saves money and time, and ensures you get optimum nutrition even when you're on the go.

2 servings

Ingredients

1 cup skim milk (or water)

¾ cup quick oats

¾ cup oat flour (store bought or made by grinding oatmeal in your blender)

2 teaspoons baking powder

½ teaspoon salt

2 packets Splenda or other sugar replacement

4 egg whites

1 teaspoon cinnamon

Nutritional Info
per serving—5 pancakes

Calories—307

Carbohydrates—47.5g

Protein—19.5g

Fat— 4.5g

Fiber—5.3g

High-Fiber Carrot-Raisin Bread

12 servings

Ingredients

1½ cup 100% whole-wheat flour

½ cup unprocessed
   wheat bran flakes

¼ cup oatmeal, dry

1 teaspoon salt

2 teaspoons baking soda

2 teaspoons pumpkin pie spice (or 1
   teaspoon cinnamon, 1 teaspoon
   nutmeg, ¼ teaspoon ground clove)

¾ cup natural unsweetened
   applesauce

6 egg whites

13 packets sugar replacement

2 cups shredded carrots

½ cup raisins

1/3 cup chopped walnuts, set aside

Nutritional Info
per serving—
1 muffin or 1 slice of bread

Calories—123

Carbohydrates—22g

Protein—5.25g

Fat—2.7g

Fiber—4g

This low-fat, high-fiber bread can be made into two small loaves, 12 muffins, or even a 9x13 cake cut into individual portions to be frozen and re-heated for a quick snack or as part of a morning meal. The recipe has been enriched with added fiber.

Directions

Preheat oven to 350 degrees. Spray two loaf pans or muffin tins with nonstick cooking spray. Combine flour, bran, baking soda, salt and spices in bowl and set aside. In large bowl, combine sweetener, applesauce and egg whites and whisk or mix with an electric mixer until well blended. Combine in dry ingredients until blended. Stir in carrots and raisins and pour into pans or muffin tins. Top with walnuts and bake approximately 30 minutes or until fork inserted in the center comes out clean. Allow to cool completely and store in airtight container or cut into pieces to be individually frozen.

Fresh Strawberry Crepes

If you're looking for something that's a little light but still loaded with protein, try these fluffy strawberry crepes. You can also substitute the strawberries with your favorite fruit or berry.

Directions

Whip all ingredients except preserves in blender. Pour batter into preheated nonstick fry pan coated with non-stick spray and cook until lightly browned. This makes about four 6-inch crepes. Fill each with one tablespoon of sugar-free preserves or cut up chunks of fresh strawberries and sprinkle with a packet of sugar replacement if desired.

Modifications

Fill crepes with one or two teaspoons fat-free cream cheese, reduced-fat Neufchatel cheese, yogurt or low-fat cottage cheese and top with fresh, chopped strawberries or sugar-free preserves. You may also wish to sprinkle lightly with chopped walnuts.

1 ser

Ingredients

6 egg whites

¼ cup low-fat cottage cheese

2 tablespoons oatmeal or oat bran

½ teaspoon vanilla

1-2 packets artificial sweetener

4 strawberries, chopped

Nutritional Info
per serving

Calories—186

Carbohydrates—15g

Protein—29g

Fat—2g

Fiber—1.9g

Ingredients

2 scoops vanilla protein*

2¼ cups oat bran

½ teaspoon salt

1 tablespoon baking powder

4 egg whites

1 cup skim milk

½ cup sugar-free maple syrup

¼ cup unsweetened, natural applesauce

½ cup frozen or fresh whole blueberries

Nutritional Info
per serving

Calories—94

Carbohydrates—12.7g

Protein—8.1g

Fat—1.29g

Fiber—2.4g

Dave's Occasional Bran Muffins

At one time or another, you may have purchased a bran muffin or box of bran muffin mix and believed you were making a sound nutritional choice. Reading the label, you may have noticed these mixes are actually full of additives, white flour, sugars and assorted chemical ingredients. This protein-fortified bran muffin is nearly devoid of simple carbohydrates, and you can make the recipe less than 20 minutes.

*The brand of protein used in this recipe contains 200 calories, 4 g carb, 44 g protein, 2 g fat, 2 g fiber.

Directions

Preheat oven to 450 degrees. Line muffin tins with paper baking cups or spray bottoms with cooking spray. Mix dry ingredients together; add remaining liquids and mix well. Fold in blueberries and pour into tins. Bake until golden brown for approximately 12 minutes or until inserted toothpick comes out clean. Cool and store in airtight container or freeze.

Modifications

If you like sweeter muffins, add two or three packets of sweetener to the recipe; if you like very moist muffins, increase applesauce to a half-cup.

Santa Fe Omelet

This egg-white omelet is packed with power, protein and a spicy little bang…just what you need to start off your busy day!

Directions

Spray large nonstick frying pan with cooking spray and sauté chicken breast, chile peppers and onions until chicken is cooked through. Push chicken off to the side of the pan and pour in eggs to make one omelet. Allow egg to cook for about one minute and spoon chicken mixture over the top of the eggs. Fold eggs over with a spatula to form an omelet and cook until egg is cooked though.   Remove omelet from the pan and top with black beans. Garnish with low-fat cheese or fat-free sour cream if desired.

IN STELLA'S KITCHEN

Did you know? The color of an eggshell carries no dietary significance. Eggshell color has nothing to do with nutritional content, quality, flavor, thickness of the shell or cooking properties. Eggshells are white or brown because the breed of chicken.

1 serving

Ingredients

3 ounces boneless, skinless chicken breast

3 egg whites plus 1 whole egg, beaten together with fork.

¼ cup canned black beans

2 tablespoons chopped green chile or jalapeno (canned is fine)

2 tablespoons diced onion (optional)

Nutritional Info
per serving

Calories—284

Carbohydrates—14g

Protein—38g

Fat—7g

Fiber—2.2g

Doc's El Paso Omelet

This is a modified version of a family favorite. If you enjoy Mexican food, you'll love this omelet. The fat has been reduced and the protein increased by replacing whole eggs with egg whites and by using a lower fat cheese than the cheddar used in the original recipe.

Directions

Mix eggs, corn tortilla, and green chile in small bowl. Spray nonstick pan with cooking spray and sauté until eggs are cooked. Top with Muenster cheese and serve. Garnish with a dollop of fat-free sour cream if desired.

In Stella's Kitchen

Storage time for eggs—Eggs keep for a long time, so buy extra whenever you see them on sale. Refrigerate eggs as soon as you get home from the store and you can safely eat them four to five weeks beyond the pack date.

1 serving

Ingredients

1 egg plus 4 egg whites, beaten

1 corn tortilla, torn into pieces

2 tablespoons chopped green chile (or salsa)

½ ounce (about ½ slice) reduced-fat Monterey jack cheese

Nutritional Info
per serving

Calories—253

Carbohydrates—16g

Protein—26g

Fat—9g

Fiber—1.4g

5

Protein Snacks

Every pound of your muscle keeps your metabolic fire stoked all day long, seven days a week. At the same time, it is healing, rebuilding and strengthening itself and needs a constant source of protein to facilitate this process. Yet, many people struggle to consume the necessary protein.

There are dark forces that beckon from corporate vending machines and lonely family pantries everywhere. They whisper tenderly, "I won't tell if you choose me. I'm sweet and cost less than a dollar,"or, "You can eat me. Just do more cardio tomorrow."

You'll be well-armed against this challenge with the protein snacks in this section. You'll find everything from real beef jerky to protein shake recipes that are devoid of the added sugar and excessive calories sometimes found in specialty-shop smoothies.

The next time you're on the go with muscles that need to be fed, grab and go with something made from this simple, but tasty section.

5

Protein Snacks

Protein Nutrition Bar

Chocolate Protein Pudding Pops

Thai Chicken Lettuce Wraps

Homemade Oven Beef Jerky (Spicy and Traditional)

Cottage Cheese Combos

Shake it Up

Peanut Brittle Shake

Iced Mocha Shake

Oatmeal Meal Replacement Shake

Banana Crème Pie Shake

Triple Chocolate Shake

Nada Colada Shake

Eggnog Shake

Troubleshooting the Protein Shake

Neapolitan Shake

Strawberries and Cream Shake

Muscle Beach Shake

The Hulk Shake

Strawberries and Chocolate Shake

Cinnamon Roll Shake

Polar Bear Shake

Peppermint Patty Shake

Amaretto Shake

Very Berry Shake

Peanut Butter Cup Shake

Orlando Orange Shake

Root Beer Float Shake

Protein Nutrition Bar

A nice snack at a mere fraction of the cost of packaged protein bars and none of the glycerin, preservatives or sugar, these low-fat bars are rich in fiber and taste great with a light spread of natural peanut butter. Served with a protein drink, they make a well-balanced meal.

Directions

Preheat oven to 325 degrees. Mix all dry ingredients in bowl and blend well. In separate bowl, combine egg whites, orange juice, applesauce and the sugar-free syrup. Blend well. Stir liquids into dry ingredients until mixed. The consistency will be thick and similar to cookie dough. Spread batter on baking sheet coated with nonstick spray, or use a 9x12 baking dish if you want a thicker serving. Bake until edges are crisp and browned. Cut into 10 bars and store in an airtight container or freeze.

*If you find you want a more moist consistency, add a little more applesauce to the recipe for softness.

**The brand of protein used in this recipe contains 200 calories, 4 g carb, 44 g protein, 2 g fat and 2 g fiber.

IN STELLA'S KITCHEN

Baking with applesauce—Did you know you can replace the oil in a recipe with an equal measure of applesauce? Applesauce will add the same moisture but not the added fat, and it won't alter the flavor.

10 servings

Ingredients

3½ cups quick oats

1½ cups powdered nonfat milk

1 cup sugar-free pancake syrup

2 egg whites, beaten

¼ cup orange juice

1 teaspoon vanilla

¼ cup natural applesauce*

4 scoops chocolate protein powder**

Nutritional Info
per serving

Calories—140

Carbohydrates—23g

Protein—15g

Fat—.5g

Fiber—4g

Chocolate Protein Pudding Pops

Next time someone around your house is craving ice cream, try this is a recipe for chocolate pudding pops, or browse through some of the other protein shake recipes for more ideas. Any of these shakes can be tweaked into "ice cream" simply by using the whole package of sugar-free pudding mix instead of the small amount called for in the recipe.

Directions

Make pudding with skim milk in accordance with producer's directions. Once pudding begins to set, stir in the protein powder and blend well. Spoon mixture into homemade Popsicle containers and freeze. For handy, bite-sized treats, use ice trays to freese these iced protein pops.

*The brand of protein used in this recipe contains 200 calories, 4 g carb, 44 g protein, 2 g fat and 2 g fiber.

IN STELLA'S KITCHEN

Make ice cream—You can make a sherbet using this same concept by using sugar-free jello and vanilla protein instead. If you don't have one of those nifty plastic homemade Popsicle gadgets, just use small plastic containers. If you do that, you'll wind up with protein ice cream (similar to ice milk) that will need to thaw a little before you can dig in—tastes great.

8 servings

Ingredients

1 box sugar-free
  chocolate pudding mix

2 cups skim milk

2 scoops chocolate protein*

½ teaspoon vanilla

Nutritional Info
per serving for added ingredients

Calories—59

Carbohydrates—7.6g

Protein—6.5g

Fat—.4g

Fiber—trace

Thai Chicken Lettuce Wraps

If you like Pad Thai or other spicy peanut chicken dishes, you'll enjoy these naturally low-carb, high-protein chicken wraps. Thai red curry paste is hot, hot, hot even in small amounts but is tamed into balance with the addition of a little natural peanut butter. The basic recipe below is great for a simple snack or made into a salad.

Directions

Spray wok with nonstick cooking spray; sauté chicken and red pepper in soy sauce until chicken juices run clear and meat is no longer pink. Add peanut butter, Thai curry paste and a small amount of water to reach desired consistency. Cook until hot and remove from heat. Serve on a bed of lettuce leaves that can be used as wraps for each piece of chicken.

IN STELLA'S KITCHEN

Party appetizer—For a more formal version of this dish, garnish the chicken strips with chopped peanuts and serve them on a large plate with red cabbage leaves, leafy greens, fresh beat sprouts, shredded carrots, rice noodles and various Asian sauces (Hoison, soy, teriyaki, hot chili oil, etc.) for dipping.

8 servings

Ingredients

1½ pound boneless, skinless chicken breast, cut into 16 strips

1 tablespoon reduced-sodium soy sauce

3 tablespoons natural peanut butter, chunky style

1½ teaspoon Thai red curry paste

16 leaves butter, red leaf or green leaf lettuce

Water or milk (to thin sauce)

Nutritional Info
per serving

Calories—123
Carbohydrates—2g
Protein—17g
Fat— 4.8g
Fiber—1.1

Homemade Oven Beef Jerky

20 servings

Ingredients

3 pounds flank steak

½ cup reduced-sodium soy sauce

2 tablespoons Worstershire sauce

3 tablespoons liquid smoke

3 teaspoons fresh cracked
  black pepper

3 teaspoons garlic powder

3 teaspoons onion powder

Nutritional Info
per serving

Calories—113

Carbohydrates—<1g

Protein—19g

Fat—3.6g

Fiber—0g

This recipe is for a basic jerky you can make even if you don't own a smoker—it bakes right into your oven. This isn't a cost-saving recipe—it can wind up costing the same as store-bought jerky—but it's better tasting, natural and won't have any of the added preservatives. You can also control the sodium level by reducing the amount in the marinade.

Directions

Remove all fat from beef. Cut beef into thin slices (quarter-inch or less) by slicing against the grain. (For a tougher, chewier jerky, slice with the grain, opposite the butcher's normal recommendations.) Combine all ingredients in a covered dish and marinate overnight in refrigerator. After marinating, preheat oven to 150 degrees and place a cookie sheet lined with paper towels on the bottom rack. Insert toothpicks into the ends of the beef strips and hang them from the top grill rack. Keep the oven door cracked slightly open so water vapor can escape. Cook for six to eight hours.

Modifications

For spicy jerky: Add three or four teaspoons of red pepper flakes to the marinade.

For teriyaki jerky: Use reduced-sodium teriyaki marinade instead of soy; add a quarter cup of brown sugar or brown sugar replacement to marinade.

IN STELLA'S KITCHEN

Affordable jerky—Wait to make this recipe until you find a large cut of flank steak, London broil or top round on sale or priced for quick clearance. These meats are perfect for making into jerky. It never hurts to ask the butcher if he's about to mark down any meat.

Cottage cheese is a great high-protein snack often overlooked for its protei[...]
half-cup serving of low-fat 2%-cottage cheese has 16 grams protein. Even [...]
monitor their carb intake can partake in it because a serving yields only fou[...]
hydrates. Here are a few flavor combinations to try with your next scoop o[...]ttage cheese.

Pepper:

Sprinkle cottage cheese with a few dashes of fresh cracked pepper.

Tapioca Pudding:

If you like tapioca pudding, try this low-carb alternative: For each half-cup serving, mix in ½ teaspoon vanilla and 1 packet artificial sweetener.

Summer Fruit:

A few strawberries, blueberries, chopped banana or pineapple on top go a long way with cottage cheese. If the fructose is a concern, try using tropical or strawberry-banana flavored sugar-free drink mix as an alternative fruit flavoring.

Crunchy Vegetable:

Adding diced red onion, chopped green pepper or even diced tomatoes makes a small but appreciable difference to a scoop of cottage cheese.

Morning Preserves:

Add 1 tablespoon sugar-free or reduced-sugar preserves per half-cup of cottage cheese.

Chocolate Mousse:

Add a half-scoop of chocolate-flavored protein (or 1 teaspoon of cocoa plus 2 packets artificial sweetener), and 1 tablespoon sugar-free chocolate instant pudding mix and whip in blender (you may need to add a little water or milk to thin it a little bit). Top with one walnut, diced finely, and chill until serving.

...ake It Up

Is there anything more basic to the diet of today's athlete than the protein shake? Fortunately, sports nutrition has advanced beyond the insoluble, bland powders of yesteryear, making it more appealing to the general public.

Day after day, the same taste can bore the tastebuds of even the most dedicated health food advocate. If not knowledgeable about alternatives, in a weaker moment you may succumb to the call of a chocolate Ding Dong.

There are protein shake recipes that call for the addition of cookies, cheesecake mix and mere tablespoons of protein powders; nutritional blasphemy! Let's not even discuss the smoothie bar chains that are adding sugary flavored powders on top of fruit concentrates and then giving you a chunk of bread to go with it.

On the ingredients...

I've focused on low sugar, low calorie, and low-to-moderate carbohydrate enhancements knowing that you generally have no trouble finding larger amounts of these on your own. My most common flavor tools are various extracts and sugar-free instant pudding. All of these can be made with low-fat milk or water and several will add slim-to-none in the way of calories.

On the quantities...

Those who desire only one scoop of protein should simply omit the second scoop from the recipes. On the other hand, those whose shakes contain more than two scoops of protein at a time will need relatively increased amounts of the ingredients listed in the recipes.

On the nutritional data...

The total nutritional value will change according to the brand and amount of protein powder and liquid used. The calorie counts are only for the added ingredients, not the protein or milk. Use this information if you are closely monitoring your calorie intake.

On the protein...

The scoop on protein...You will hopefully be pleasantly surprised by the extensive variety of protein shakes included in this section. If you are unfamiliar with using protein for a quick nutritional supplement between meals, my suggestion is that you start with a basic whey protein powder or a "time-released" blend made with various types of proteins. Vanilla is probable the most versatile flavor because you can easily change its flavor. It can be purchased at health food stores, mail order catalogs and internet nutritional supplement websites. Even with shipping costs, you will usually get the best deal online or via mail order as opposed to a large chain store.

Peanut Brittle Shake

I discovered this delicious favorite quite by accident as I sat staring at my "boring" vanilla protein powder, wanting something sweet. It mimics peanut brittle only in taste; it won't send your blood sugar soaring, and it's a fun way to get some healthy unsaturated fat.

Directions

Add all ingredients to blender, blend and serve. I like to add the peanut butter last so it stays chunky; others prefer to blend it sooner for a smoother consistency.

1 serving

Ingredients

2 scoops vanilla protein

1 tablespoon sugar-free instant butterscotch pudding mix, dry

1 tablespoon natural peanut butter, chunky

8 ounces cold water or lowfat milk

3–6 ice cubes

Nutritional Info
for added ingredients (excludes milk and protein powder)

Calories—108

Carbohydrates—6g

Protein—4g

Fat—8g

Fiber—1g

Iced Mocha Shake

Anyone for a great shake to sip during the morning traffic jam or to rev up the engine prior to an early morning workout?

Ingredients

- 2 scoops chocolate protein (or 2 scoops vanilla plus 1 tablespoon unsweetened cocoa powder)

- 1 tablespoon instant coffee granules or 1½ teaspoon ground coffee

- 1 teaspoon unsweetened cocoa powder (optional)

- 8 ounces coffee (cooled), cold water or low-fat milk

- 3–6 ice cubes

Directions

Add all ingredients to blender, blend and serve. If you like a stronger mocha flavor, you'll want a little cocoa powder or more coffee. Use milk if you're fond of lattes or love the frozen coffee confections served at popular modern coffee shops.

IN STELLA'S KITCHEN

Saving money—Speaking of specialty coffee, there is an economical way to make a flavored cup of coffee. Instead of using sugar-loaded syrups, their expensive sugar-free counterparts or specially flavored coffee, try a few drops of vanilla, almond, mint, amaretto or any other extract. Extracts, found near the spices in most grocery stores, will flavor a cup of coffee at a fraction of the cost without sabotaging your diet.

Nutritional Info
for added ingredients (excludes milk and protein powder)

Calories—13

Carbohydrates—2g

Protein— 0g

Fat—0g

Fiber—0g

Oatmeal Meal Replacement Shake

1 serving

This is a homemade meal replacement shake designed to provide the complex carbohydrates, protein and good fat necessary to extend your energy stores. If your day is expected to be hectic, why not double it up and take half of the shake to work to ensure you don't skip a meal as you hustle from here to there?

Directions

Add all ingredients to blender, blend and serve. If you're short on time, use dry oatmeal.

Ingredients

½ cup dry measure oatmeal, cooked in water and cooled

2 scoops vanilla protein

3 dashes cinnamon

⅛ cup sugar-free maple syrup or equivalent amount brown sugar re placement

1 tablespoon chopped almonds (or flaxseed oil or natural peanut butter)

12 ounces water or low-fat milk

Nutritional Info
for added ingredients (excludes milk and protein powder)

Calories—215

Carbohydrates—33g

Protein—7g

Fat—7g

Fiber—5g

Banana Crème Pie Shake

Ingredients

2 scoops vanilla protein

½ medium banana

½ teaspoon vanilla

2 tablespoons sugar-free, instant banana or vanilla pudding mix

½ tablespoon walnuts

8 ounces cold water or low-fat milk

3–5 ice cubes

A crustless version of the banana lover's favorite pie, this can also be enjoyed by those on carb-restrictived diets by making the suggested modifications. The walnuts in the recipe provide essential fats and a hint of pie crust flavoring.

Directions

Add all ingredients to blender, blend and serve.

Modifications

Low-carb version: Omit the half-banana and the sugar-free, instant pudding mix and use one-quarter teaspoon banana extract as flavoring instead. For this, you can subtract 56 calories and 14 grams of carbohydrates.

Nutritional Info
for added ingredients (excludes milk and protein powder)

Calories—113

Carbohydrates—21g

Protein—2g

Fat—0g

Fiber—3

Triple Chocolate Shake

This is for my friends at Chocoholics Anonymous. Many people simply add chocolate syrup to their shakes, but using real cocoa imparts a more natural, deep chocolate flavor without adding sugar. This triple dose of chocolate might satiate those primal cravings for chocolate without destroying your day's calorie goals.

Directions

Add all ingredients to blender, blend and serve. If you like dark chocolate, use an additional half to full tablespoon of cocoa powder for a deeper chocolate flavor.

1 serving

Ingredients

2 scoops chocolate protein

½ tablespoon unsweetened cocoa powder

1-2 tablespoons sugar-free chocolate or sugar-free white chocolate instant pudding mix

8 ounces water or lowfat milk

3–5 ice cubes

Nutritional Info
for added ingredients (excludes milk and protein powder)

Calories—22

Carbohydrates—4g

Protein—0g

Fat—0g

Fiber—.8g

Ingredients

2 scoops vanilla protein

½ cup pineapple-orange juice

¼ teaspoon rum extract

¼ teaspoon coconut extract (or 2 tablespoons real coconut)

1 packet artificial sweetner

8 ounces cold water or lowfat milk

5 ice cubes

Nutritional Info

for added ingredients (excludes milk and protein powder)

Calories—61

Carbohydrates—15g

Protein—0g

Fat—1g

Fiber—0g

Nada Colada Shake

Try serving this protein-packed umbrella-topped Pina Colada knock-off at your next pool party and see how many people you can convert from milk shakes to power-packed protein drinks.

Directions

Add all ingredients to blender, blend and serve. Then garnish with umbrella, sunglasses and Hawaiian shirt.

Modifications

Low-carb version: Use a sugar-free pineapple-orange drink mix instead of real fruit juice.

Eggnog Shake

This is a unique substitution for the traditional fat-laden eggnog served during the holidays. The extracts and spices mimic the taste of eggnog, and the sugar-free instant pudding captures the rich creaminess without adding the buttermilk fat in the traditional recipe for eggnog.

Directions

Add all ingredients to blender, blend and serve. This one really works best with milk and the use of sugar-free pudding to help duplicate the consistency of real eggnog.

If you wish to exclude the raw egg, subtract 75 calories, 5 grams fat, 1 gram carb, and 6 grams protein from the nutritional totals; most health experts advise against raw egg consumption, while many athletes continue the practice.

1 serving

Ingredients

2 scoops vanilla protein

1 raw egg (optional)

2 tablespoons sugar-free vanilla pudding mix (optional)

¼ teaspoon rum extract

2 dashes cinnamon

2 dashes nutmeg

1 dash Butter Buds or ½ teaspoon artificial butter flavor

8 ounces lowfat milk or cold water

3 ice cubes

Nutritional Info
for added ingredients (excludes milk and protein powder)

Calories—100

Carbohydrates—7g

Protein—6g

Fat—5g

Fiber—0g

Troubleshooting The Protein Shake

We've all got our own quirky taste and texture preferences, even for simple protein shakes. Here are a few tips you may find useful in preparing your favorite protein shakes.

If your shake...

is too thin: Try adding a few ice cubes, frozen fruit, or a tablespoon of sugar-free instant pudding mix to thicken it.

is too thick: Some protein mixes have guar gum or other artificial thickeners in them. To use up less-favorable protein powders, you can make shakes using only a half-serving, mixing in a regular whey protein to cover the protein gap.

is not creamy enough: Try using a tablespoon of sugar-free pudding mix if you make your shakes with water or milk. If you use milk, you can try using milk with higher fat content (1 or 2% instead of skim). Low-carb dieters or those not concerned with low calorie counts can add some half and half—magic!

is not "foamy" or frothy enough: Extend the whip time in the blender to fluff the shake.

won't dissolve: Solubility are usually related to the the particular brand of protein. Your best option is to first blend your liquid and ice and slowly add the protein to the blender. Look for an "instantized" protein that blends easily to avoid the problem all together.

is not sweet enough: Add a packet or two of Splenda or a small piece of banana. Fructose (fruit sugar) is 70% sweeter than sucrose (table sugar); a small piece of banana or other fruit goes a long way in providing sweetness.

has weak vanilla flavor: A ½ teaspoon of imitation vanilla flavor or ¼ teaspoon vanilla extract will enhance the vanilla flavor without adding calories. Alternatively, you could add a tablespoon of sugar-free instant vanilla pudding.

has weak chocolate flavor: A teaspoon of real cocoa powder will give you a nice chocolate flavor without adding the sugar that comes with using chocolate syrup. This is a great idea for those who only purchase one flavor of protein at a time because you can add cocoa to vanilla protein to make rich chocolate shakes.

sticks to blender glass: Always add the liquid to your blender or shaker first. When blending thicker shakes, try pouring the protein into the blender as it whirls or lightly pushing the powder down with a spoon to ensure it mixes.

is "to go": To cut down on dishes and make a handy "to go" shake, you may be able to use a pint or quart Mason jar in place of your blender pitcher. Simply remove the blending attachment from the pitcher; if it twists onto the jar (like a jar cap), it will work. Put your drink ingredients into the jar, twist on the blending assembly, turn the jar top-down onto the blender and hit the switch. Voila!

Neapolitan Shake

The flavor of this shake is reminiscent of my childhood summers. My sister Olivia would scoop us each a bowl of Neapolitan ice cream and then we'd smash, stir and swirl it into a delicious smooth mixture that combined all the flavors. You can also throw a banana in this one for a melted mock-banana split.

Directions

Add all ingredients to blender, blend and serve.

In Stella's Kitchen

One flavor fits all—If you've only got the budget for one flavor of protein, buy vanilla. It's the easiest flavor to manipulate and still drink plain. Transform two scoops of vanilla protein into chocolate flavored by adding one or two teaspoons of cocoa powder or into strawberry with a few frozen strawberries.

1 serving

Ingredients

2 scoops strawberry protein (or 2 scoops vanilla plus 3 frozen strawberries)

1 tablespoon unsweetened cocoa powder

½ teaspoon vanilla

8 ounces water or lowfat milk

3-6 ice cubes

Nutritional Info

for added ingredients (excludes milk and protein powder)

Calories—25

Carbohydrates—2.8g

Protein—1g

Fat—.5g

Fiber—1.4g

Ingredients

2 scoops strawberry protein (or 2 scoops vanilla plus 4 strawberries)

3 fresh or frozen strawberries

1½ tablespoon sugar-free vanilla pudding mix

1 dash Butter Buds or other butter-flavored seasoning

¼ teaspoon vanilla

8 ounces cold water or low-fat milk

3–5 ice cubes

Nutritional Info
for added ingredients (excludes milk and protein powder)

Calories—36

Carbohydrates—9g

Protein—0g

Fat—0g

Fiber—0g

Strawberries and Cream Shake

This shake has a fresh, wonderful strawberry and crème taste that will please those with even the most refined and discriminating palates. Strawberries are loaded with Vitamin C and antioxidants, so feel free to grab a couple and dip them in your shake.

Directions

Add all ingredients to blender, whip and serve—in a parfait glass garnished with a strawberry! I like extending the whip time on this shake to give it a nice, creamy "mouth feel."

Muscle Beach Shake

Muscle Beach has a light citrus taste that offers a taste of California right in your kitchen. This one has lots of variety and flavors—just like the people seen strolling down the Venice Beach boardwalk.

Directions

Add all ingredients to blender, blend and serve.

Modifications

Low-carb version: Omit fruit juice and banana and use one-half teaspoon strawberry-orange-banana sugar-free drink mix instead. Subtract all nutritional counts as this alternative will not add any caloric or nutritional value to the liquid and protein powder used.

1 serving

Ingredients

2 scoops vanilla protein

½ cup orange juice

3 strawberries

½ medium banana

8 ounces cold water or lowfat milk

3–5 ice cubes

Nutritional Info
for added ingredients (excludes milk and protein powder)

Calories—122

Carbohydrates—30g

Protein—2g

Fat—0g

Fiber—2g

The Hulk Shake

Ingredients

2 scoops vanilla protein

1½ tablespoons sugar-free pistachio
  pudding mix

1 mint leaf or a few drops
  peppermint extract (optional)

1 few drops green food coloring
 (optional)

8 ounces cold water or low-fat milk

3–5 ice cubes

I came up with this pistachio-flavored shake for my son one busy morning—he loved it because it was green, and he spent the rest of the day doing lat spreads that "ripped his shirt." I loved it because it only added 19 calories to my protein shake. If you're over the age of six, omit the lat spreads and head to the gym for a weight workout.

Directions

Add all ingredients to blender, blend and serve. This tastes great without the mint so don't worry if you don't have it on hand. The shake is a light green even without the food coloring but if you want it deep green, like The Hulk, you'll need a few drops.

Nutritional Info
for added ingredients (excludes
milk and protein powder)

Calories—19

Carbohydrates—5g

Protein—0g

Fat—0g

Fiber—0g

Strawberries and Chocolate Shake

Imagine how romantic this one can be when served to your significant other in a glass with two straws. Double up on the strawberries for extra vitamin C.

Directions

Add all ingredients to blender, blend and serve. I let this one whip a little longer to develop the smooth feel of chocolate.

Ingredients

1 scoop strawberry protein
(or 1 scoop vanilla plus 2 extra strawberries)

1 scoop chocolate protein
(or 1 scoop vanilla plus 1 teaspoon cocoa powder)

3 fresh or frozen strawberries

1 tablespoon sugar-free chocolate pudding mix (optional)

8 ounces cold water or low-fat milk

3–5 ice cubes

In Stella's Kitchen

Loving touch—Garnish this with a strawberry slice and dust of cocoa or a teeny bit of grated chocolate. You can even make a few chocolate curls by running a vegetable peeler over warm chocolate.

Nutritional Info
for added ingredients (excludes milk and protein powder)

Calories—25
Carbohydrates—6g
Protein—0g
Fat—0g
Fiber—.6g

Cinnamon Roll Shake

This is a yummy favorite of mine that tastes like the icing on a cinnamon roll without the pitfalls of the sugar.

Directions

Add all ingredients to blender, blend and serve.

1 serving

Ingredients

2 scoops vanilla protein

½ teaspoon vanilla (optional)

¼ teaspoon ground cinnamon

1 tablespoon sugar-free
  vanilla pudding
 (optional, for creaminess)

1 packet Splenda
  or other artificial sweetener

A few dashes Butter Buds or
  ¼ teaspoon imitation butter-
  flavor extract

3 ice cubes

Nutritional Info

for added ingredients (excludes milk and protein powder)

Calories—25

Carbohydrates—5g

Protein—0g

Fat—0g

Fiber—0g

Polar Bear Shake

The Polar Bear tastes like a liquid candy cane but will not require a follow-up visit to the dentist. There are no added calories or nutrition in the ingredients; this is just a fast flavor change.

Directions

Add all ingredients to blender, blend and serve.

IN STELLA'S KITCHEN

Holiday fun—Swirl in a few drops of red food coloring after preparing and it becomes a holiday "candy cane." Serve under mistletoe.

1 serving

Ingredients

2 scoops vanilla protein

¼ teaspoon peppermint extract

8 ounces cold water or low-fat milk

4 ice cubes

Nutritional Info
for added ingredients (excludes milk and protein powder)

Calories—0

Carbohydrates—0g

Protein—0g

Fat—0g

Fiber—0g

Peppermint Patty Shake

Ingredients

2 scoops chocolate protein

¼ teaspoon peppermint extract

1 teaspoon cocoa
(optional, use if you like a deeper
chocolate flavor)

8 ounces cold water or lowfat milk

3–5 ice cubes

This is a chocolate mint-flavored protein shake made by adding only a trace of calories to a regular chocolate shake. Reminds me of those innocent-looking cookies you can buy once a year outside the grocery store. Given the chance, many of us could eat a whole row of them. Instead of actually doing that, try whipping this minty chocolate dream up after a good workout.

Directions

Add all ingredients to blender, blend and serve.

Nutritional Info
for added ingredients (excludes milk and protein powder)

Calories—6

Carbohydrates—.8g

Protein—.4g

Fat—.1g

Fiber—.5g

Amaretto Shake

The nutty flavor of Amaretto liqueur is delicious; here's an alternative that's not full of empty calories. In fact, there are no added calories in the recipe. You could also add sugar-free lemonade mix to this and you'd have the smoothie equivalent of an Amaretto Sour.

Directions

Add all ingredients to blender, blend and serve.

Modifications

A few almonds can be added if you're looking for some added healthy fat.

Ingredients

2 scoops vanilla protein (chocolate or strawberry tastes good, too)

½ teaspoon almond extract

¼ teaspoon rum extract

8 ounces cold water or low-fat milk

3–5 ice cubes

Nutritional Info
for added ingredients (excludes milk and protein powder)

Calories—0

Carbohydrates—0g

Protein—0g

Fat—0g

Fiber—0g

Very Berry Shake

The Very Berry shake is a delicious way to boost your fiber and Vitamin C intake. Just three ounces of berries give you almost three grams of fiber and 17mg of natural vitamin C. You can find frozen berry blends at the store or buy them fresh in season and freeze in your own small, snack-sized baggies.

Directions

Add all ingredients to blender, blend and serve.

IN STELLA'S KITCHEN

Protein "yogurt"—If you like fruity yogurt but the carb addition wreaks havoc with your diet, try adding a tablespoon of sugar-free pudding mix to the Very Berry recipe and extending the whip time. Reduce the water or low-fat milk to half-cup and add one ice cube at a time until you have a lucious consistency.

1 serving

Ingredients

2 scoops strawberry protein
(can substitute vanilla)

½ teaspoon vanilla (optional)

3 ounces frozen berry blend
(strawberries, blueberries,
raspberries)

8 ounces cold water or low-fat milk

3 ice cubes

Nutritional Info
for added ingredients (excludes milk and protein powder)

Calories—53

Carbohydrates—13.4g

Protein—.42g

Fat—.26g

Fiber—2.62g

132

Peanut Butter Cup Shake

This is an easy one—I'm surprised to discover it's not a regular for everyone. Use natural peanut butter, smooth or chunky. The recipe calls for a tablespoon but if you use more or less, it will still come out fine. If you want more carbohydrates, add a banana.

Directions

Add all ingredients to blender, blend and serve.

Ingredients

2 scoops chocolate protein
(or 2 scoops vanilla plus 1 heaping tablespoon cocoa powder)

1 tablespoon natural peanut butter

8 ounces cold water or low-fat milk

3–5 ice cubes

Nutritional Info
for added ingredients (excludes milk and protein powder)

Calories—95

Carbohydrates—3g

Protein—4g

Fat—8g

Fiber—1g

Orlando Orange Shake

Ingredients

2 scoops vanilla protein
or use chocolate for a "chocolate orange" flavor

¼ teaspoon strawberry-orange flavored sugar-free drink mix

1 tablespoon sugar-free vanilla pudding mix

8 ounces cold water or low-fat milk

3 ice cubes

This is an orange cream-flavored tribute to the great state of Florida. When made with only water, the taste of this calls rainbow sherbet to mind at the cost of only 13 added calories!

Directions

Add all ingredients to blender, blend and serve.

Modifications

If you're looking for additional carbohydrates, simply use a half-cup orange juice and real strawberries.

Nutritional Info

for added ingredients (excludes milk and protein powder)

Calories—13

Carbohydrates—3g

Protein—0g

Fat—0g

Fiber—0g

Root Beer Float Shake

Experience a root beer float without the guilt—about 13 calories will be added to your regular protein shake depending on how you choose to prepare this recipe. Sugar-free instant vanilla pudding has been added to imitate some of the creaminess of ice cream but you can leave it out and still enjoy this special treat.

Directions

Add protein, ice, water and pudding mix to blender. Mix well. Pour into large cup and add the desired amount of diet root beer.

1 serving

Ingredients

2 scoops vanilla protein

1 tablespoon sugar-free instant vanilla pudding mix

4 ounces cold water or low-fat milk

3 ice cubes

About 3 ounces diet root beer

Nutritional Info
for added ingredients (excludes milk and protein powder)

Calories—13

Carbohydrates—3g

Protein—0g

Fat—0g

Fiber—0g

Vegetable Basics

Eating vegetables is the best way to get the vitamins and minerals your body needs to maintain itself and to grow strong. Here are some delicious vegetable basics you can prepare quickly to replenish your body's carbohydrate, fiber and other micro-nutrient needs.

6

Vegetable Basics

Green Beans Almondine

Garlic Smashed Potatoes

Steamed Broccoli with Lemon and Garlic

Papa Bear's Sweet Potato "Fries"

Grilled Asparagus

Greek Vegetable Medley

Herbed New Potatoes

High-Protein "Fried" Rice

Baked Winter Squash Bisque

Popeye's Spinach and Rice Hot Dish

Broiled Italian Vegetables

Gary's Macho Gazpacho

Fresh Salad 101

Selecting greens

Iceberg lettuce contains little nutritional value because it consists mainly of water. Select greens that are dark and leafy, like green leaf, red leaf, romaine or mixed baby greens for your salads instead. Leafy greens offer valuable fiber, which many of our diets are lacking.

Storing greens

Make a big base salad to use all week. When you get home from the store, wash, dry and tear the leaves. Place a damp paper towel on top of the greens and store them in a covered bowl so they will stay fresh. Use this as a base and add various items to it as your desire and schedule permits.

Make a meal

Add chicken, tuna, beef, egg whites, favorite vegetables, lean ground beef and salsa, leftover fajitas or other items to your green salad base throughout the week for an easy meal.

Best dressed

Heaviness can overtake a great meal when the greens are drenched in ranch dressing. You can easily make your own olive oil and vinegar dressing, or even a vinaigrette.

To make basic vinaigrette

Whisk one tablespoon Dijon mustard, one-half tablespoon olive oil, and three tablespoons Balsamic vinegar and season to taste with pepper.

To make flavored vinaigrette

Simply substitute different types of vinegars or add herbs to the basic recipe. Red wine and raspberry vinegars, finely minced garlic or shallots, basil, rosemary, thyme or oregano are just a few options you can try in your own vinaigrette.

Green Beans Almondine

Ingredients

4 cups fresh green beans,
   washed and cut in half

1 tablespoon olive oil

½ tablespoon Italian herbs
   (basil, rosemary, parsley)

1 ounce slivered almonds

Salt and fresh ground pepper

People often eat only canned or frozen green beans. While opening a can is easy, the full flavor potential of the green beans is not experienced. Try this variation, but make the effort to use fresh green beans. This recipe is well-suited for family dinners.

Directions

Preheat oven to 450 degrees. Toss green beans, herbs and olive oil together in large bowl. Place on baking sheet and top with almonds. Bake 8–10 minutes, turning once, or until almonds begin to visibly toast.

Nutritional Info
per serving

Calories—77

Carbohydrates—6.3

Protein—2.1g

Fat—4.8g

Fiber—3.1g

Garlic Smashed Potatoes

Who says you need butter to make really good mashed potatoes? These garlic-inspired potatoes have a full flavor without the bath of sodium or fat-laden gravy.

Directions

Place potatoes in medium saucepan and cover with water. Add skim milk and garlic and bring to a boil over medium high heat. Reduce heat to medium and cook until potatoes are tender (about 20 minutes). Drain potatoes, reserving the cooking liquid for later use. Add sour cream and parsley and smash potatoes to desired consistency, using reserved cooking liquid to thin as desired. Season to taste with fresh ground pepper and salt.

In Stella's Kitchen

Leave the potato skins on—If you've never tried mashed potatoes with the skins on, you're in for a treat. Not only does leaving the skins on save time, it provides you with the added fiber, protein and vitamins and minerals present in the skin. Flavor increases as a side bonus.

4 servings

Ingredients

1¼ pounds unpeeled
red potatoes, cut in chunks

1/3 cup skim milk
(or reduced-sodium chicken broth)

¼ cup reduced-fat sour cream

8 cloves garlic, peeled and crushed

1 teaspoon dried parsley
(or 2 teaspoons fresh parlsey)

Salt and fresh ground pepper to taste

Nutritional Info
per serving

Calories—146

Carbohydrates—28.1g

Protein—4.2g

Fat—1.9g

Fiber—2.4g

Steamed Broccoli with Lemon and Garlic

Ingredients

5 cups fresh broccoli, cut

2 lemons, cut into wedges

3 cloves minced garlic
(or 2 teaspoons of water-packed minced garlic)

1 teaspoon toasted sesame seeds
(optional)

Fresh ground pepper to taste

Fresh broccoli was not eaten in my home as a child. When I started to eat healthy, I made an adult decision to try it… without cheese sauce. I had a dish simiar to this in a restaurant and was disappointed to discover I'd missed out on 23 years of eating this amazing vegetable. It's since become a favorite.

Directions

Steam or microwave broccoli a few minutes before meal-time. Squeeze lemon juice over broccoli, add garlic and toss. Sprinkle with sesame seeds if desired.

Modifications

You can pan toast the sesame seeds for a tasty flavor addition. Try toasting a cup to store in the cupboard for several months of use.

Nutritional Info
per serving

Calories—166

Carbohydrates—22g

Protein—11g

Fat—3.4g

Fiber—1.25g

IN STELLA'S KITCHEN

Broccoli…vegetable extraordinaire—If you could only eat a single vegetable, broccoli would be a wise choice. Just a single 25-calorie cup of broccoli is loaded with almost three grams of fiber, 137% of the minimum daily Vitamin C requirements, and a little calcium!

Papa Bear's
Sweet Potato "Fries"

4 servings

The sweet potato is lower on the glycemic index than the regular potato. This makes the sweet potato a good choice of carbohydrate for those who monitor their blood sugar levels. While baked sweet potatoes are great too, this provides an interesting variation with more fiber to keep you full.

Ingredients

1 pound sweet potatoes, cut into fry wedges

Garlic powder

Nonstick cooking spray

Directions

Preheat oven to 350 degrees. Spray sweet potatoes with cooking spray. Bake for 30–35 minutes, flipping them once during cooking. Sprinkle with garlic powder.

Modifications

Instead of garlic powder, sprinkle cooked sweet potato fries with cinnamon and Splenda for a sweet treat.

Nutritional Info
per serving

Calories-121

Carbohydrates—27.5g

Protein—1.9g

Fat—.3g

Fiber—3.4g

Grilled Asparagus

Ingredients

1 pound asparagus,
washed and dried

Garlic salt or powder

Fresh ground pepper to taste

Asparagus can be a little pricey depending on time of year, but this makes a great high-fiber sidedish when grilled on an outdoor barbeque or counter-top grilling appliance.

Directions

Lay asparagus lengthwise across grill and sprinkle with seasonings. Cook for about five minutes or until the asparagus becomes sufficiently al dente. Be alert—don't overcook these tender vegetables.

Nutritional Info
per serving

Calories—66

Carbohydrates—10.3g

Protein—5.2g

Fat—.5g

Fiber—4.8

Greek Vegetable Medley

Eggplant is extremely hearty for a vegetable due to its fiber content. If you've never eaten it, it behaves a little like a Portobello mushroom, absorbing the liquids and flavors like a thirsty sponge. You can serve this as side or perhaps in a whole-wheat pita stuffed with chicken breast. This vegetable medley can be mixed together and broiled instead of prepared as below. You may want to try mixing in Greek olives after cooking, or toasting the pine nuts before adding them to the dish.

Directions

Sauté onion and peppers in light olive oil until tender. Add eggplant and cook for about five minutes, stirring occasionally. Add all remaining ingredients except pine nuts and vinegar and bring to a boil. Cover and simmer until eggplant is very tender (10–15 minutes). Remove from heat and stir in pine nuts and vinegar.

6 servings

Ingredients

2 medium red bell peppers, chopped and seeded

2 medium eggplants, cut in chunks

1 medium red onion, chopped

¾ cup reduced-sodium tomato sauce

¼ cupwater

1 tablespoon light olive oil

1½ tablespoon red-wine vinegar

2 ounces pine nuts

Salt, fresh ground pepper and red pepper flakes to taste

Nutritional Info
per serving

Calories—102

Carbohydrates—11.7g

Protein—2.8g

Fat—5g

Fiber—3.5g

Herbed New Potatoes

Ingredients

1½ pounds new potatoes

¼ cup chopped shallots

1 tablespoon olive oil

1 teaspoon dried Rosemary
(or 1 tablespoon fresh herbs)

1 teaspoon dried basil
(or 1 tablespoon fresh herbs)

Salt and fresh ground pepper
to taste

These potatoes taste best baked, but you can also steam or boil the potatoes and then season them for a quick serving of carbohydrates. The recipe calls for shallots, a rather mild member of the onion family usually found in the produce section near the garlic.

Directions

Preheat oven to 350 degrees. Toss all ingredients together and cook in a baking dish sprayed with nonstick spray. Bake about one hour until potato skins begin to crisp. If you're in a hurry, simply steam or boil the potatoes and season before serving.

Nutritional Info
per serving

Calories—175

Carbohydrates—34g

Protein—3.1g

Fat—2.8g

Fiber—3.2g

High Protein "Fried" Rice

This is a great recipe to prepare when you have a small amount of leftover rice or are closely monitoring your carbohydrate intake. This version is much more healthy than what's found in restaurants and it's been protein enhanced in order to make it a one-dish meal.

Directions

Cook egg whites in nonstick skillet and set aside. Spray pan with nonstick cooking spray and sauté onion, garlic and a dash of soy until garlic is lightly browned. Add rice and chicken and cook until warm. Add broth and egg whites and cook until hot. Season to taste with ground pepper and a little salt.

4 servings

Ingredients

1½ cup cooked brown rice, cooled

6 egg whites, beaten

8 ounces cooked chicken breast (or shrimp)

¼ cup green onion (or yellow onion, if preferred)

2 cloves garlic, peeled and finely diced

2 tablespoons reduced-sodium chicken broth

Dash of reduced-sodium soy

Salt and fresh ground pepper to taste

Nutritional Info
per serving

Calories—185

Carbohydrates—17.8g

Protein—23g

Fat—2.4g

Fiber—1.5g

Ingredients

3 pounds butternut squash
(or a mixture of your favorite winter
squashes)

3¼ cups reduced-sodium
chicken broth

8 cloves garlic, peeled and finely
diced (or 3 ½ teaspoon prepared
minced garlic)

1 medium yellow onion, chopped

1 teaspoon dried rosemary

Salt and fresh ground pepper to taste

Nutritional Info
per serving

Calories—75

Carbohydrates—11.9g

Protein—4.8g

Fat—1g

Fiber—2g

Baked Winter Squash Bisque

If you grow a vegetable garden, here's a nice way to enjoy your bountiful harvest. The recipe calls for butternut squash, but you can use a mixed variety of your favorites. On cold winter days when you're enjoying the indoors, try cozying up with this nutritious and easy-to-prepare soup. The smell of the squash baking is wonderful!

Directions

Preheat oven to 400 degrees. Wash and dry the squash, cut in half length-wise and scoop out the seeds. Pierce the squash several times with a knife and bake for 50 minutes or until very soft. In a large soup pot, combine garlic, onions and a quarter-cup of the broth and bring to a boil. Scoop squash from skins and add to soup pot. Stir in remaining broth. Bring all ingredients to a boil over medium-high heat. Reduce heat, cover and simmer for 20 minutes. Puree cooked ingredients in a blender or food processor and return to soup pot; add rosemary and blend well. Season with salt and pepper to taste and cook until hot. Serve with a dollop of fat-free sour cream or nonfat plain yogurt if desired. Store the remainder in individual servings to enjoy later.

Popeye's
Spinach and Rice Hot Dish

This is a strong-to-the-finish "hot dish" modified from its original high-fat version. Consider adding chicken breast chunks, shrimp or other protein to this for a more complete one-dish meal.

Directions

Preheat oven to 350 degrees. Combine all ingredients in large bowl. Spray casserole dish with nonstick cooking spray and spoon in mixture. Bake 35 minutes.

IN STELLA'S KITCHEN

Cooking rice—One of the most common problems with cooking rice is uneven cooking. If you routinely notice the rice towards the bottom cooks while the top portion remains raw, try using a heavier or tighter fitting lid to prevent the steam from escaping too quickly. Alternatively, you can place a piece of aluminum foil over the pan before covering it with a lid.

4 servings

Ingredients

2 cups brown rice, cooked (or wild rice, if preferred)

½ cup reduced-fat mild cheddar cheese

1 egg plus 6 egg whites

4 tablespoons parsley, chopped

2 green onions, chopped

1 pound fresh spinach washed, drained, chopped

Nutritional Info
per serving

Calories—204

Carbohydrates—27.6g

Protein—15.6g

Fat— 3.6g

Fiber—5g

Broiled Italian Vegetables

4 servings

Ingredients

2 medium zucchini, cubed

1 medium eggplant,
  cut in large chunks

1 red bell pepper, cut in strips

6 cloves garlic,
  peeled and finely diced

2 tablespoons olive oil

3-4 leaves fresh basil, chopped
  (or substitute 1 teaspoon dried
  basil or "Italian herb" blend)

Salt and fresh ground pepper
  to taste

These are great broiled in the oven or grilled, and served with chicken or fish.

Directions

Preheat broiler or oven to 500 degrees. Toss vegetables, garlic, herbs and olive oil together in a large bowl. Broil vegetables on a foil-lined baking sheet until they begin to brown. Turn vegetables once and continue broiling until slightly charred.

Nutritional Info
per serving

Calories—166

Carbohydrates—22g

Protein—11g

Fat—3.4g

Fiber—1.25g

Gary's
Macho Gazpacho

Gazpacho is a cold, spicy vegetable soup that originated in Spain. This version has been boosted with protein and has a jalapeno added for extra kick. Omit the shrimp for a vegetarian version, or even omit the jalapeno to remove some of the heat that makes this a "macho" gazpacho.

Directions

Score an "X" in the base of each tomato using a paring knife. Blanch the tomatoes by dipping them into boiling water for one minute and then plunging them in an ice bath. Peel away the skin and chop finely. Mix all ingredients together and season to taste. Use two to three cups of chilled water to thin the soup to a desired consistency. Cover and refrigerate for two to three hours. Serve chilled. Gazpacho keeps well in fridge for about five days.

8 servings

Ingredients

3 pounds ripe tomatoes

1½ pound cooked salad shrimp

2 large cucumbers, diced

1½ green bell pepper, chopped

1 jalapeno, seeded and diced

4 cloves crushed garlic

1½ tablespoon black olives, chopped

½ cup red wine or rice vinegar

¼ cup olive oil

2 cups reduced-sodium tomato sauce

1 large yellow onion, chopped

4 green onions, chopped

Nutritional Info
per serving

Calories—233

Carbohydrates—18.4g

Protein—20.8g

Fat—8.6g

Fiber—4.3g

7

Safe Sauces

Prepared sauces and toppings are generally formulated for convenience, not for the purpose of better nutrition and health. For the health-conscious person, acceptable sauces and toppings can be very limited if one does not have the knack of cooking from scratch. Whether the concerns are adequate protein, reduced sodium or sugar, or the reduction of fat, there is no reason why these constraints should limit the food experience to boring, lifeless meals. Here are just a few examples of quick sauces and marinades you can prepare to beat blandness, and which can be easily modifed to meet your specific dietary concerns.

7

Safe
Sauces

Quick, Fresh Tomato Sauce

This is a fast, light sauce you can make in a few minutes. It's lower in sodium and sugar, yet provides a fuller flavor than traditional canned sauce. Try this tossed with grilled chicken or shrimp and served with a side of pasta or rice.

Directions

Sauté garlic in light olive oil over medium heat until lightly browned. Add tomatoes and cook until hot. Toss in your choice of herbs for an additional minute and remove from heat. Season to taste with fresh cracked pepper and salt.

*Use two teaspoons of dried herbs if you do not have fresh herbs on hand.

In Stella's Kitchen

Fresh herbs year-round—Freeze leftover herbs (or the excess herbs grown in a summer garden) for a treat of their unmatched taste year-round. Remove leaves from the main stem, rinse and dry. Place leaves flat on a long sheet of plastic wrap and roll them up. Store in the freezer and when called for in a recipe, simply snip a small piece off the end and unroll.

4 servings

Ingredients

4 large ripe tomatoes, chopped

2 cloves garlic, pressed or finely chopped

4 tablespoons fresh Italian herbs, chopped (try basil, oregano, parsley, or arugula)*

1 tablespoon light olive oil

Salt and fresh ground pepper to taste

Nutritional Info
per serving

Calories—68

Carbohydrates—8.5g

Protein—1.5g

Fat—4g

Fiber—trace

6 servings

Ingredients

1 8-ounce can reduced-sodium tomato sauce

2 cups water

¼ cup Worcestershire sauce

½ medium yellow onion, finely minced

¼ cup red wine vinegar

3 teaspoons chili powder

2 teaspoons paprika

1 teaspoon fresh ground pepper

Nutritional Info
per ¼-cup serving

Calories—20

Carbohydrates—5g

Protein—.5g

Fat—0g

Fiber—0g

Barbeque sauce is a wonderful marinade for grilling or serving over chicken, beef and shrimp. However, a mere two tablespoons can cost you nine grams of sugar and 20% of your daily sodium allotment. This homemade barbeque sauce can be made quickly from common kitchen ingredients and does not contain the added sugar or high sodium of store-bought sauces.

Directions

Combine all ingredients in saucepan and bring to a full boil.Cover and simmer for at least 20 minutes. Allow to cook uncovered until reduced to desired thickness. Remove from heat and store in covered container until ready to use.

Suggested uses

Marinade, grilling sauce or sauce base

For sandwiches: Use slices of high-fiber, whole grain bread to make the following homestyle sandwiches.

Sloppy Joes: Mix with one pound extra lean ground beef

BBQ Chicken: Mix with shredded chicken breast

BBQ Beef: Mix with shredded top round beef

Pico De Gallo

This is one family recipe that didn't require any modification—Pico De Gallo is a fresh salsa you can make to accompany fajitas or for use as a south-of-the-border topping on steak, chicken breast or omelets.

Directions

Mix all ingredients together in medium bowl. Pretty simple! Refrigerate until ready to serve.

Modifications

Add a half-cup diced avocado to recipe.

Ingredients

2 large ripe tomatoes, chopped

½ medium onion, diced

1 fresh jalapeno, diced finely

1½ teaspoon fresh cilantro, chopped

¼ teaspoon garlic powder

Juice from a few lemon wedges (optional)

Salt and fresh ground pepper to taste

Nutritional Info
per serving

Calories—25

Carbohydrates—5.75g

Protein—1g

Fat—.25g

Fiber—0

Fresh
Summer Vegetable Sauté

Ingredients

4 roma tomatoes, chopped

1 medium green bell pepper, diced

1 medium zucchini, cut into strips

1 medium yellow squash,
  sliced and quartered

½ medium red or yellow onion,
  sliced

3 cloves garlic, pressed or finely
  chopped

5 leaves fresh basil, chopped*

1 tablespoon light olive oil

3 tablespoons Balsamic vinegar

Salt and fresh ground pepper
  to taste

Nutritional Info
per serving

Calories—50

Carbohydrates—7g

Protein—1.1g

Fat—2.5g

Fiber—1.2g

This is a very light vegetable sauté modeled after a sauce at a popular Italian restaurant chain. You can make this with any vegetables you have on hand, so don't limit yourself to what you see listed here. This is sauté goes well with grilled chicken or shrimp.

Directions

Sauté garlic in light olive oil over medium heat until lightly browned. Add vegetables and Balsamic vinegar and cook until hot. Add basil and season to taste with fresh cracked pepper and salt.

* Use two teaspoons of dried basil if you do not have fresh basil on hand.

IN STELLA'S KITCHEN

Which olive oil should I buy? Lighter colors of olive oil are more refined and have a lighter, less distinguishable taste. Use a light or extra-light olive oil if you intend to use it as a basic cooking oil. To impart a deeper, more distinctive taste to your Italian cooking or dressings, use a darker green, extra-virgin olive oil; use a lower heat when using darker olive oils.

Low-Fat Alfredo Sauce

Real Alfredo sauce is made with excessive amounts of cream, butter and cheeses that healthy eaters should most often avoid. This is a lighter version of Alfredo made with lighter cheeses in place of the traditional high-fat version.

Directions

Puree ricotta, cottage cheese and skim milk in blender. Add cheeses and garlic and cook in medium saucepan over medium heat until cheeses are melted. Stir in the parsley and serve with pasta. Season to taste with fresh cracked pepper and salt.

 * Use two teaspoons of dried parsley if you do not have fresh herbs on hand.

Modifications

Macaroni and Cheese: Replace Mozzarella and Parmesan with reduced-fat cheddar and serve over pasta noodles.

Vegetable Alfredo: Add slices of fresh red and green pepper, sun-dried tomatoes or roasted red peppers.

IN STELLA'S KITCHEN

Fresh garlic—You can drastically reduce the amount of salt required to season food by using fresh garlic. Buy small jars of minced garlic to keep on hand to use in lieu of fresh garlic cloves—tastes much better than garlic powder or garlic salt.

6 servings

Ingredients

½ cup fat-free ricotta cheese

½ cup fat-free cottage cheese

¼ cup skim milk

¼ cup grated Parmesan cheese

1/3 cup reduced-fat Mozzarella cheese, shredded

4 cloves garlic, minced or pressed

¼ cup fresh parsley, minced

Fresh cracked pepper to taste

Nutritional Info
per serving

Calories—95

Carbohydrates—3.8g

Protein—12.2g

Fat—3.3g

Fiber—trace

Ingredients

1 large ripe tomato

1 jalapeno pepper

1 Serrano chile pepper

4 Anaheim green chile peppers
   (try to select flat ones)

Garlic powder, salt and fresh
   ground pepper to taste

Nutritional Info
per serving

Calories—59

Carbohydrates—13g

Protein—3g

Fat—1g

Fiber—1g

Wito's
Skillet Roasted Green Chile

Every time I smell this, I think of my dad explaining to me that I should never add flour to green chile because the fresh roasted green chile peppers are degraded into a gooey gravy. If you make it fresh, there is no reason to mask the natural roasted flavors with starchy flour that adds calories but no nutritional value. Try it as a salsa, marinade or stew base.

Directions

Preheat a nonstick skillet over medium-high heat. Place chile peppers in skillet and allow vegetable skins to blacken, turning when necessary. Once pepper skins have blackened, allow vegetables to cool. Vegetables should be soft and the skin should peel off easily. Remove skin from all vegetables and carefully seed and de-vein the chile peppers. Puree all ingredients in blender, adding water to reach desired thickness. Season to taste and keep refrigerated until ready to use.

IN STELLA'S KITCHEN

Storing tomatoes—Store tomatoes with the stem side down to help them keep longer.

Sun-Dried Tomato and Spinach Sauté

This quick and light sauce provides a slight twist on the standard, quick tomato sauce. Add cooked chicken breast and serve with a side of orzo, risotto or Arborio rice for a full meal.

Directions

Sauté garlic and onions in light olive oil over medium heat until lightly browned. Add tomatoes and broth and cook until hot and tomatoes are soft. Slip in basil and spinach for an additional minute and remove from heat. Season to taste with fresh cracked pepper and salt.

*Use two teaspoons of dried basil if you do not have fresh herbs on hand.

4 servings

Ingredients

1 10-ounce can fat-free chicken broth

1 3-ounce package sun-dried tomatoes, dry, chopped (or a can of salt-free stewed tomatoes, drained and chopped)

3 cloves garlic, pressed or finely chopped

1/3 cup red onion, sliced

½ tablespoon light olive oil (optional)

5 leaves fresh basil, chopped *

6 leaves fresh spinach, washed and torn

Salt and fresh ground pepper to taste

Nutritional Info
per serving

Calories—51

Carbohydrates—15g

Protein—1.5g

Fat—3.7g

Fiber—trace

Chihuahua Chile Rojo

8 servings

This easy-to-make red chile is made by boiling the dried pods of the red chile often seen hanging in Mexican restaurants. I grew up to the scent of "chile de ristra" boiling on the kitchen stove for enchiladas, but I've since found healthier uses for it. Chile is naturally low in calories and has even been added to some thermogenic products to raise metabolism. It's a flavorful marinade or sauce for grilled chicken or any type of lean beef.

Ingredients

1 bag New Mexico chile pods (Chile de Ristra)

3 cloves garlic, pressed or finely chopped or garlic powder

Salt to taste

Water

Directions

Crack off tops of chile pods and discard. Shake pods to remove seeds. Boil the chile peppers in water until they reconstitute and skins are soft (about 20 minutes). Drain. Puree chile pods along with garlic in half-cup of water. Continue adding water until the sauce reaches desired consistency.

IN STELLA'S KITCHEN

Can't take the heat? The heat of any chile, dried or fresh, lies in the veins and seeds, so remove them before preparing your favorite dishes.

Nutritional Info
per serving

Calories—32g

Carbohydrates—7.6g

Protein—1.1g

Fat—.22g

Fiber—2.12g

Salsa Picante

With barely any calories, this fresh salsa goes a long way in flavoring food. It's great with fajitas, on top of your favorite omelet, or in place of salad dressing.

Directions

Combine all ingredients in large bowl and season to taste. Refrigerate in covered bowl or jar to use as needed. You may wish to puree the canned tomatoes first if you don't want a chunky consistency.

IN STELLA'S KITCHEN

Green tomatoes—Green tomatoes will ripen in four or five days if wrapped in newspaper and stored in a cool dry place. If you need them to ripen quicker, place them in a brown paper bag in indirect sunlight

15 servings

Ingredients

1 large ripe tomatoes, chopped

2 16-ounce cans salt-free crushed tomatoes

1 medium onion, diced

1 fresh jalapeno peppers, seeds removed and finely diced

2 fresh Anaheim green chile peppers, diced

2 teaspoons fresh chopped cilantro (optional)

½ teaspoon garlic powder

Juice from one lemon

Salt and fresh ground pepper to taste

Nutritional Info
per serving

Calories—18

Carbohydrates—4.1g

Protein—.8g

Fat—.13g

Fiber—.1g

Roasted Red Pepper Sauce

One of the keys to maintaining a healthy diet year round is to allow yourself to experience a wide range of flavors to keep your taste buds entertained. This fresh sauce provides that variety and is great served over pasta or brown rice and chicken breast.

Ingredients

1 10-ounce can fat-free reduced-sodium chicken broth

1 large ripe tomato, chopped (or one can reduced-sodium stewed tomatoes, drained and chopped)

4 cloves garlic, pressed or finely chopped

1 8-ounce jar roasted red peppers (packed in water), drained and chopped

½ tablespoon light olive oil (optional)

5 leaves fresh basil or arugula, chopped *

Salt and fresh ground pepper to taste

Directions

Sauté garlic in light olive oil over medium heat until lightly browned. Add tomatoes, broth and peppers and cook until hot. Add your choice of herbs for an additional minute and remove from heat. Season to taste with fresh cracked pepper and salt.

*Use two teaspoons of dried herbs if you do not have fresh herbs on hand.

Modifications

Mediterranean: Omit basil and sprinkle final dish lightly with crumbled feta cheese.

Spicy: Add one or two teaspoons red pepper flakes.

Nutritional Info
per serving

Calories—42

Carbohydrates—5.25g

Protein—1.75g

Fat—2.25g

Fiber—trace

Guacamole Lijera
(Lean Guacamole)

One of the more interesting parts of cooking healthy is the discovery of substitutions that allow us to continue enjoying our favorite foods. This is one of those strange ideas that really works! The fat in the avocado is not necessarily unhealthy except in excess. This recipe stretches out the guacamole and has just 3.3 grams of fat per serving, allowing the enjoyment without the guilt.

Ingredients

1 medium avocado,
  peeled and cubed

1¼ cup frozen green beans, thawed

¼ cup fat-free sour cream

3 tablespoons chunky salsa

1 small tomato, diced

2 cloves garlic, pressed or minced

Juice of one lemon

Fresh ground pepper to taste

Directions

Puree avocado, green beans, sour cream, garlic and lemon juice in blender or food processor. Transfer guacamole base to bowl and stir in the salsa and chopped tomato. Season to taste with fresh cracked pepper and salt.

Modifications

You can add finely diced red or yellow onion to the guacamole for added flavor.

Nutritional Info
per serving

Calories—52

Carbohydrates—5.9g

Protein—1.1g

Fat—3.3g

Fiber—1g

The Kitchen Toolkit

The intent of this cookbook has been to demonstrate that making better food choices and cooking healthy doesn't mean sacrificing flavor, time, or even taming your ethnic food preferences. These last few pages are a comprehensive toolkit designed to encapsulate the most important concepts within this cookbook's recipes and suggestions.

You may already know how to cook and eat healthy and perhaps have simply learned a few facts and obtained new recipes to revise shamelessly into your own masterpieces. Perhaps you were a skeptic who was a bit unsure about taking time to read a cookbook, and already you're enjoying the gifts of time you find that comes with using smart cooking techniques.

I smile when I think of the careful readers who meticulously measured every ingredient while hunched over the pages ("What's the secret ingredient she said to put into every dish again?"). I nod knowingly to the men and women who may now be following the same troubling path I spent many years upon. I understand your conflicts with enjoying good food, and I hope you see that in these pages.

You have spent a little time in Stella's Kitchen strengthening your faith that good food and good health can be a part of your life forevermore. Now it's time for you to strike out on your own to the grocery store and make choices based on the concepts and food formulations that piqued your interests. And now it's time for *you* to make your own kitchen a special place where a healthier, happier, stronger body begins its day.

8

Kitchen Toolkit

Fast Fuel: Healthy Cooking Tips for Busy Lives

Today's world moves at a fast pace. To accommodate busy schedules, fast-food restaurants have cropped up at an alarming pace. Many personal records and physical excellence lie dormant within those who believe they cannot cook healthy with limited time, and choose to succumb to their busy schedules. Maybe you work two jobs or have a family, but you don't need to resign yourself to the couch. With just a little planning and advance preparation, you can keep fast-food runs and kitchen time to a minimum.

1. Cook in bulk. Set aside two one-hour periods per week to cook staples to use all week. For example, store a covered container of cooked chicken that you can re-heat plain or turn into a quick stirfry. Cooked chicken can be refrigerated two to three days; save time just cooking once to cover several days.

2. Freeze in individual portions. Store pre-measured or weighed foods in individual portions. Plastic snack-size bags hold approximately a half-cup of cooked rice or dry oatmeal so keep these pre-measured packs on hand. When you have leftovers, immediately freeze them in plastic compartment trays with snap-on lids. For example, save leftover rice, broccoli and chicken for a wonderful homemade frozen meal, ready for your busy workday.

3. Flash marinate. Keep those taste buds entertained so you aren't tempted by the desire to eat out. When you get back from the store, cut and measure out your chicken or beef into your specific-size portions. Measure each portion and toss in spices, lemon juice, salsa or any other marinade and freeze. When you take the meat out to thaw, it will simultaneously marinate as it defrosts.

4. Precut. Wash and precut broccoli and lettuce heads when you get home from shopping to store in a big bowl. A damp paper towel across the top of the greens and a lid will help them keep all week. You can add more vegetables to the salad if you have time or just use the greens as a base for many kinds of salads during the week.

5. Pack meals the night before. Packing your meals the night before ensures you won't be in a scramble for an emergency meal at a fast-food joint, or even have to drink protein shakes or dry tuna all day. You can even prepare your breakfast so that all you need to do is warm it up in the morning.

6. Maintain a supply of emergency food, especially protein. Keep a small stock of emergency protein like canned tuna, canned chicken and protein powder at work, in your car, in your gym bag, at home and anywhere you may find yourself without quality food. You may also wish to keep oatmeal and natural peanut butter on hand for carbohydrates and fats.

Body Budget: 11 Rules for the Cook on a Tight Budget

One of the greatest misconceptions about making better food choices is that it somehow "costs too much" to eat right. When you factor in sick days, prescriptions, doctor visits and frequent meals that come with eating a wayward diet you may see that, it costs more if you don't eat smart. If you incorporate a few of these basic strategies, eating for better health can be both a sound economic decision and a valuable investment in your quality of life.

1. Buy carbohydrates in bulk. Buy oatmeal, brown rice, potatoes and beans in bulk. Always buy the larger economy-sized containers when they're on sale. Stick to regular rice (not instant) for additional savings.

2. Never buy full price meat products. Meat can be frozen for several months so you should only buy it when it is on sale. Watch newspaper circulars for teaser meat specials designed to draw in foot traffic. Tuna, chicken breast and lean beef cuts are ALWAYS on sale someplace. Look for "reduced for quick sale" or other value-pack deals to save even more.

3. Shop using a grocery list. A grocery list will help you avoid buying things on impulse and misappropriate grocery funds for things you don't need. If you stick to it, it will also keep your daily calorie count stable.

4. Buy generic. Let go of your brand and store loyalties. Shop by best value, not brand name. Some stores even list a cost per ounce on the shelf label. Use it to help you select the best brand and size of the item being purchased—it pays to compare.

5. Limit purchases of toiletries, cleaning products and pre-packaged foods. This includes overpriced diet foods. These are also things that are often on sale and can be stored a long time, so don't buy them at full price. You do not need separate cleansers for everything in the house or to buy what you can make quickly at a fraction of the cost. You do, however, need quality groceries to fuel your body—divert more of your grocery budget towards nutritious food.

6. Don't throw anything away. Freezing leftovers like extra rice, sauces or leftover pasta in half-cup snack baggies will save money and time. Save leftovers in individual plastic dishes for healthy, fast meals or work lunches.

7. Primarily shop the outer ring of the store. Most of the nutritious, fresh food is located in the outer ring of the store. The closer you get to the epicenter, the nearer you are to more dangerous foods like chips, soda, too many cans and packages, and finally, cake mixes and ice cream. Big tip: Don't take your cart down the center aisles.

8. Make your own salads. Bagged lettuce and pre-cut vegetables cost three to four times the price of un-packaged versions. You can tear two heads of dark, leafy lettuce or cut up a few pounds of broccoli in less than one minute for the same grab-and-go convenience.

9. Limit experimentation with nutritional supplements, especially if you have just started an exercise program. Buy one flavor of protein at a time and only when it is on sale. Rather than be sucked in by an employee's sales pitch, do a little bit of online research before deciding to purchase any supplements. Buy what you need to keep training hard but don't go crazy buying products that promise the unbelievable results that only consistent diet and persistent efforts can deliver.

10. Don't smoke, and don't drink heavily. A monthly expense budget that includes a carton a week habit of smokes or two nights at the bar is worth 50 pounds of sale-priced boneless, skinless chicken breast and at least a few years of waking up and seeing the sun.

11. Eat clean…at home. Learn to cook. Stay home. Use your savings towards next Tuesday's meat sale or to cover a monthly gym membership.

Cooking Lean: Substitution and Replacements

Instead of using...	*Try...*
Beef—70-85% lean ground or chuck	92% or leaner ground beef or 92% lean ground turkey or buffalo
Bread crumbs, as breading or to mix with meat	Unprocessed bran flakes and mixed with oat flour, crushed all bran cereal flakes, oat flour or oatmeal
Butter	Butter replacement product, Butter Buds, imitation butter flavor extract
Cheese	Reduce amount and use part-skim mozzarella or reduced fat or nonfat cheese
Chicken—whole bird or dark meat	Equal amount boneless, skinless breast or whole breasts with skin removed
Egg—1 whole	2 egg whites or 1 tablespoon cornstarch dissolved in 3 tablespoon of water
Flour—white	Oat flour, 100% whole wheat flour, soy flour
Gravy	Omit or thin with water to aus jus consistency
Kool-aid or juice	Crystal Light
Milk—in cereal	Vanilla or strawberry protein powder mixed with water
Milk—whole, in cooking or baking	Nonfat or low-fat milk or just water

Instead of using...	Try...
Oatmeal—flavored packets	Natural oats and chopped fruit or sugar-free preserves (see "Eat Your Oatmeal," page 91)
Oil—in baking	Equal amount of unsweetened applesauce
Oil—in cooking	Omit or try reducing by half or two-thirds
Oil—when sautéing	Wine, broth, lemon, apple or orange juice
Salt	Garlic, chile, onion or lemon
Sour cream	Fat-free plain yogurt or nonfat sour cream
Soy sauce	Reduced-sodium soy or reduced-sodium chicken or beef broth
Sugar—brown	Diabetic pancake syrup
Sugar—white	Sucralose (Splenda) or other artificial sweetener of choice, or 1 teaspoon mashed banana per tablespoon of sugar being replaced
Syrup—pancake or maple syrup	Sugar-free (diabetic) pancake syrup. In cereal, try artificial sweetener and a few drops of maple extract
Syrup—chocolate	Cocoa powder and sucralose to taste
Syrups—flavored (such as that used in coffee)	Sugar-free syrup or sucralose and a few drops vanilla extract or other extract of choice

Fit Flare: A Guide to Healthy Marinades and Seasonings

Italian

Plain tomato sauce, spaghetti sauce, diced tomatoes, basil, parsley, or rosemary, fresh ground pepper

Balsamic vinegar, basil, fresh ground pepper

Any type of vinaigrette or Italian dressing

Lemon juice, parsley, capers

Mediterranean

Oregano, onions, garlic, tomato

Onion, oregano, lemon, nonfat plain yogurt

Garlic, onion, lemon, dill

Indian

Red or yellow curry powder, onions, garlic, ground cardamom, nonfat plain yogurt

Asian

Thai chili paste, lemon juice, garlic

Garlic, green onion, reduced-sodium soy stretched with water, sesame seeds

Thai chili paste, natural peanut butter, lime juice

Southwest/Tex-Mex

Chili powder, lime juice

Onion, garlic, lime, cilantro

Sugar-Free BBQ Sauce (see recipe on page 156)

Green pepper, onion, salsa

Salsa

Chopped green chili or jalapeno, diced tomato

Eastern European

Chicken broth (reduced sodium), canned tomatoes, paprika

French

Onion or shallot, wine, rosemary, thyme or tarragon

Still My Favorite:
Guidelines for Modifying Family Favorites

Somewhere along the line, many of us began to associate love and comfort with Grandma's five-cheese lasagna or Mom's deep-fried chicken. When we make the decision that our bodies, our training, or real life problem solving is more important than food fixes, we sometimes fail to notice the simple things that can be done to modify family favorites so they can be included in our diets more often. Here are a few simple guidelines to help you tighten up an old family recipe.

1. Reduce or omit fats. You can usually reduce the amount of oil in regular recipes by at least a third to a half without affecting taste. Use leaner cuts of meat (such as chicken breast instead of the whole bird) and experiment with limited amounts of added oils. Try sautéing with broth, vegetable juice, citrus juices and nonstick cooking spray.

2. Decrease simple carbohydrates. Sugar and other useless carbohydrates sneak into everything from our breakfast cereals to the gum we chew. Use sugar replacements or cut the amount of simple carbohydrates used in recipes by one-third to one-half. Think about more complex and fibrous carb sources you can use instead. This will have an added benefit of helping you feel full while maintaining your energy levels.

3. Substitute, substitute, substitute. See chart on page 172-3 for common replacements.

4. Bulk up with vegetables. When you remove excess pasta, sauce or other ingredients from a dish, but know you'll want a full plate, just add extra fibrous vegetables like broccoli or green peppers.

5. Go naked. Learn to enjoy the texture, tastes and aroma of food that isn't drenched in gravies or blanketed in cheese. Think about things you can do to keep the food in a dish closer to a natural state.

6. Get fresh. Use fresh or fresh-frozen ingredients as opposed to dried, processed, canned or heavily-salted prepared foods chock-full of preservatives. The taste, scent and nutritional value fresh herbs and vegetables add to cooking will be unmatched. Good, fresh, simple food doesn't need to soak in butter.

7. Understand aesthetic value. Use different colors and textures of vegetables, or two opposing flavors in a dish. (See the chicken pasta salad on page 53 as an example where green, red, black and white create a visual; soft and crunchy items create a sensation; and the aroma of fresh basil overpowers any sense that there are not hunks of cheese and pepperoni tossed into the salad.

8. Spice it right. Use vegetables that are naturally sweeter, like red peppers or tomatoes; spicier like chile peppers; bold like garlic and onion; or, tangy like lemon juice, to minimize the need for heavy sauces, sugars and salts.

9. Increase the protein. While you're busy skimming saturated fat and empty sugar calories, think about getting adequate protein from food sources and to increase the amount of protein in a recipe where possible.

10. Mind portions. Sometimes all you need to do is remember portion sizes. The four cups of rice on your plate at a restaurant is a cheap way of tricking you into thinking you got a good deal.

11. Get real. There are some foods (like my chocolate chip cookies) that are simply better left to occasional splurge days.

Shopping Lean: The Grocery Cart
Photocopy for your use

Proteins

- [ ] Boneless, skinless chicken breast
- [ ] Tuna *(water packed)*
- [ ] Fish *(salmon, seabass, halibut)*
- [ ] Shrimp
- [ ] Extra lean ground beef or ground round
- [ ] Ribeye steaks or roast
- [ ] Top round steaks or roast *(stew meat, london broil, stir fry)*
- [ ] Top sirloin *(sirloin top butt)*
- [ ] Beef tenderloin *(filet, filet mignon)*
- [ ] Top loin *(NY strip steak)*
- [ ] Flank steak *(stir fry, fajita)*
- [ ] Eye of round *(cube meat, stew meat, bottom round, 96% lean ground round)*
- [ ] Ground turkey, turkey breast slices or cutlets *(fresh meat, not deli cuts)*

Complex carbohydrates

- [ ] Oatmeal *(old fashioned or quick oats)*
- [ ] Sweet potatoes *(yams)*
- [ ] Beans *(pinto, black, kidney)*
- [ ] Oat bran cereal
- [ ] Brown rice
- [ ] Farina *(cream of wheat)*
- [ ] Multi-grain hot cereal
- [ ] Pasta
- [ ] Rice *(white, jasmine, basmati, arborio, wild)*
- [ ] Potatoes *(red, baking, new)*

Fibrous carbohydrates

- [ ] Green leafy lettuce *(green/red leaf, romaine)*
- [ ] Broccoli
- [ ] Asparagus
- [ ] String beans
- [ ] Spinach
- [ ] Bell peppers
- [ ] Brussels sprouts

Other produce and fruits

- [ ] Cucumber
- [ ] Green or red pepper
- [ ] Onions
- [ ] Garlic
- [ ] Tomatoes
- [ ] Zucchini
- [ ] Fruit *(if acceptable on diet)*: bananas, apples, grapefruit, peaches, strawberries, blueberries, raspberries, lemons

Healthy fats

- [ ] Natural style peanut butter
- [ ] Olive oil or safflower oil
- [ ] Nuts *(peanuts, almonds)*
- [ ] Flaxseed oil

Dairy and eggs

- [ ] Low-fat cottage cheese
- [ ] Eggs
- [ ] Low or nonfat milk
- [ ] Yogurt
- [ ] Reduced-fat cheese

Condiments and miscellanea

- [ ] Fat-free mayonnaise, mustard
- [ ] Reduced-sodium soy sauce
- [ ] Balsamic vinegar
- [ ] Salsa
- [ ] Salt-free seasonings *(chili powder, lemon pepper, Mrs. Dash)*
- [ ] Steak sauce
- [ ] Bragg's liquid aminos
- [ ] Splenda *(sucralose)*
- [ ] Sugar-free maple syrup
- [ ] Extracts *(vanilla, almond, etc)*
- [ ] Crystal light, diet soda, bottled water

Resource Appendix

Online Resources

Food Nutrient Databases and Calculators
USDA Nutrient Database for Standard Reference
www.nal.usda.gov/fnic/cgi-bin/nut_search.pl

Glycemic Index for Selected Foods
www.mendosa.com/gi.htm

Nutrition Analysis Tool 2.0
www.nat.uiuc.edu

Recipe Calc4.0 (downloadable trial version available)
www.RecipeCalc.com

Temperature and Measurement Conversion Tools
www.microimg.com/science/index.html
www.geocities.com/tempconverter

Personal Food Logs
www.fitday.com
www.dietpower.com
www.health-fitness-tips.com/downloads
www.workoutsforwomen.com/foodjournal1.asp

Agencies, Organizations, Councils and Boards
US Department of Agriculture:
www.usda.gov

US Food and Drug Administration
www.fda.gov

American Egg Board:
www.aeb.org

National Turkey Federation
www.turkeyfed.org

National Cattleman's Beef Association
www.beef.org

National Agricultural Statistics Service
www.usda.gov/nass

FDA Guide to Understanding Food Nutrition Labels
www.cfsan.fda.gov/%7Edms/foodlab.html

Center for Nutrition Policy Promotion
www.usda.gov/cnpp

Prepared and Fast Food Facts and Nutritional Analysis
www.kenkuhl.com/fastfood
www.fatcalories.com
www.preparedfoods.com

Food Safety
www.extension.iastate.edu/foodsafety

Recipes, Cooking Technique Tips
www.healthyeating.net/he_1.htm
www.bodybuilding.about.com/library/essentials/fitfood/blmusclefood.htm
www.lowfatcooking.about.com
www.all-recipes.com
www.cooking.com
www.eat.epicurious.com
www.foodfit.com
www.theturkeystore.com/recipes.asp

The Food and Cooking Network Cooking Tips
www.e-cookbooks.net/tips.htm

Ethnic and Specialty Food Suppliers
www.ethnicgrocer.com
www.embasa.com
www.goya.com

Sports Nutrition and General Nutrition
www.sportsmedicine.about.com
www.davedraper.com/nutrition-contents.html
www.nutrition.about.com

Cooking and Nutrition Books
Weight Watchers Complete Cookbook and Program Basics

Sugar Free Toddlers by Susan Watson

Betty Crocker's New Choices Cookbook

The George Foreman Lean Mean Fat Reducing Grilling Machine Cookbook by George Foreman and Connie Merydith

The Food Lover's Companion, 2nd ed., by Sharon Tyler Herbst

Fats that Heal, Fats that Kill by Udo Erasmus

Natural Hormonal Enhancement by Rob Faigin

Downloadable Cookbooks:
www.e-cookbooks.net/elibrary

Index

STELLA JUAREZ

Stella Juarez, B.A., is a single mother, athlete and freelance writer. She has applied and developed her artistic and technical skills in a variety of professions, but her expression is best displayed in her cooking expertise. She contributes cooking and fitness material to various exercise and food magazines and websites, and she excels in teaching others the skills of healthy food preparation.

Stella is a bodybuilding enthusiast whose fitness adventures began far from the dumbbell rack—she started walking in her early efforts to shed 50 pounds. Walking led to recreational running and eventually she completed a marathon, raising money for a leukemia patient in the Vancouver International, 2000. Along the way she grabbed a barbell, learned how to squat, press and curl, and embarked on a lifelong love affair with muscle and the iron.

Ms. Juarez is About.com's Guide for bodybuilding; her information-packed About.com website can be found at www.bodybuilding.about.com.

You can reach Stella by email via her publisher at sjuarez@ontargetpublications.com.